EX LIBRIS

Dave Jones

PRACTICAL WESTERN
TRAINING

With a Foreword by Randy Steffen

New York

The author wishes to give his special thanks to Sandy Cross and Jalma Shaeffer, who typed the manuscript; to Ken Serco and Mac Jones (who is really Mrs. D. J.) for taking the pictures the author didn't take himself; and to the Quarter Horse Journal *for permission to include in revised form certain material that originally appeared on its pages. The jacket photo is by L. Grant Peeples.*

Published by ARCO PUBLISHING COMPANY, Inc.
219 Park Avenue South, New York, N.Y. 10003

First ARCO Printing, 1972

Library of Congress Catalog Card Number 68-57463
ISBN 0-668-02537-9

Manufactured in the United States of America

To the Memory of
ARTHUR ("POPS") KONYOT
*Horseman, showman and trainer extraordinary,
and my poker-playing buddy*

Here is Randy Steffen, the well known artist-historian-cowboy, cutting cattle on the Colombian Paso mare Yocunda.

Foreword

Many books have been written about training horses. Unfortunately, not all the people who have written books about training horses are qualified to train horses, much less write about training, or for that matter, anything else. But I suppose the same can be said for every subject about which books are written.

Books are the keys that unlock the treasure chests of knowledge. Books written by people who are not qualified are deadly weapons, for they plant false information in the minds of those who thirst for knowledge and are starved for the infinite details that make knowledge useful and rewarding.

Skill in working with horses can never be attained just by reading. A man who desires to acquire the skill, and the pleasure such skill affords, must put into practice the things that good books on horse training tell him. But first he must have confidence that the book or books he has selected have been written by horsemen whose knowledge is sound and the result of long experience based on methods known to have withstood the tests of time. Horse training is one of man's oldest skills, and as with all skills, there are correct ways to apply it . . . and there are ways that are less than correct.

Any book that attempts to tell its readers how to accomplish some specific task is most difficult to write in a style that remains free of boring repetition and an air of superiority. But here you will find a book to surprise and delight you! Not only will you learn exactly how to go about training a western horse to do many things . . . you'll find yourself relishing every word of it! Dave Jones' ability as a horseman is equaled by his ability to tell

5

you how to train a horse and entertain you through every sentence of it!

It's been my pleasure to know Dave for a long time, and I've followed his career from one end of the cow country to the other. I take off my hat to him as a master horseman . . . one of the most serious I've ever known . . . and as a master at telling others how to train horses without boring them for a single moment. And you'll take off *your* hat to him when you see your horse responding to the things you'll learn in the pages of this book!

RANDY STEFFEN

Fort Pierce, Florida

Preface

I have always liked horses. I think this is a prime requisite for a horse trainer, though there seem to be a lot of horse trainers who don't like horses. If you ask me, any guy who is constantly clubbing the horses he's supposed to be training doesn't like horses. And if he has this disdain for horses, he should be in some other line of work, for the man must be leading a miserable life and so are his horses.

Some guys "knock and spur" a handle on their horses; that's one way. You won't find that kind of stuff in this book. Sure, sometimes you have to get a little rough with a rough horse, and I'll tell you how to do this. But I won't tell you how to beat up a horse.

Some little guys take out their resentment at the world by beating on their horses. "Here's this great big horse and here's little me. I can tie up this horse, beat the head off of him and he can't do a thing about it." This is no good. I don't like any man who beats up a horse.

I guess I should tell you about my qualifications so you can decide for yourself whether or not you want to read this book. There are a lot of books about training a horse, and the reader should be selective.

My mother foaled me in 1927 in the little town of Columbus Grove, Ohio. I had already had some riding experience as she rode quite a bit and even did some jumping when she was carrying me. My dad had always been with horses, though most were the kind you hitched to a buggy.

I can't remember a time when I didn't have a pony or a horse.

7

But no one knew much about training a saddle horse back there then, and most horses were a sorry-going lot.

When World War II came along, people started getting some money in their pockets and the pleasure horse came into his own. I was right amongst them. I got my first job breaking horses for pay in, I believe, 1943.

I really thought I was salty. Other kids were playing baseball and football; I was breaking horses. I was short on science but long on determination. Those horses ended up broke, but they were what we later used to call "sop and tater" horses. I sure couldn't teach them what I didn't know.

After serving some Navy and college time, I headed west. I'd decided life would be a miserable thing without horses, so I'd best get with it. I had a period of drifting around, trying to learn a business with no one to teach me.

Heck, I used to forefoot a colt, hobble him, tie up a hind foot, saddle, slip on a hackamore and go for a ride. I remember once breaking fourteen colts to ride, with not a one in the bunch knowing how to lead. I'd ride up to a gate, get off to open it, get on, ride through, and get off to close it. I was like all kids out there. If a colt didn't buck, he was not worth owning.

I was riding for the Hatchet Cattle Company when I met my first California cowboy. This guy didn't like my horses or the way I handled them. He was strong with the talk about what a dandy hand he was. I hated every hair on his head. The longer I knew him the more he'd tell me about what he could do. He'd trained every horse on the West Coast that I could name. He'd worked with every top trainer. He'd doubled for all the top western stars and called them by their first names. He could make saddles, braid hackamores, engrave silver, outrope the best and ride any horse any time. I had never before met such an egotistical man and was glad when roundup was over and we were laid off to go our separate ways.

That winter I got a job caretaking on a dude ranch and breaking a few horses. This was up above Cripple Creek, Colorado— but on my first trip to town the first guy I see is this blowhard. He had just married a young girl from Cripple Creek and had no job or money. He asked how I was doing, and I told him that I was slowly starving to death. He said that he was in the same fix and thought he'd move in with me so we all would have each other's company while starving. And I just stood there and let him move in.

He sure could sell a bill of goods. We soon had a hundred horses to break. He'd made a deal with a local horseman and we were up to our ears in colts—and what a surprise I got! He could do all he said he could. What a hand he was! There was old Spanish tradition behind every move he made. I learned more from him in two weeks than I'd learned in two years before. Those colts worked in a fashion that was unbelievable to me. He showed me how to pick a colt to slide him, how to double a rank colt to make him pay attention and how to make a colt handy by working in circles and figure eights.

He'd rope a colt while sitting on an old pack horse. His loop would snake out and throatlatch a colt; he'd throw some slack up in the air to give himself time to dally, and have the colt snubbed and saddled in no time. He'd tell me what to do, and I was really training colts for the first time in my life.

The Korean War split us up and I've not seen him since. I write so much about this episode in my life because he showed me how little I knew when I thought I was a top hand. Since then I've tried not to get that "know-it-all" attitude. I've tried to keep an open mind to learn new things, as one constantly does when handling horses.

I've worked in California, Colorado, Nebraska, South Dakota, Pennsylvania, Ohio, Virginia and now in Florida. I've learned from all those states. In Virginia I met the famous circus rider, Artur Konyot. We became great friends and I was amazed at what his dressage horses could do. Much of the dressage training was like the California methods I'd learned; the terminology was different, but the results were the same. Mr. Konyot would say that a horse must be "collected" before he can do much. The Californians would say that he has to be "up in the bridle." He got me more interested in leg aids, suppleness and, of course, collection, which is what dressage is all about.

I've had my own training stable at various times, and the horses that were brought to me were a *real* education—you *must*

produce results or you don't eat. What can you do when the horse
brought to you is a runaway, a bucker, a rearer, a sulker or a
horse that doesn't have any *try?* A trainer has a couple things that
he can rely on. The first is a glib tongue. I told myself early in
my training life that I wouldn't use this aid. I would be brutally
honest with my customers.

So if the glib tongue isn't used, results must be accomplished.
Every horse is different; there's no set pattern for training. Each
bad habit that the horse has must be analyzed, and a plan must
be formulated to deal with the habit. If such-and-such plan doesn't
work, the trainer must keep on until he finds one that does, and
gets some results. But this plan might not work on another horse
with a similar habit. This kind of scheming about how to outwit
the bad-habit horse is constant, but it is rewarding for the person
who really wants to learn the training business. I guess I'll still
be learning when I'm eighty, if I'm around that long.

There's a reason for everything a horse does. They aren't such
terribly mysterious animals, on average. (Some may be almost
past figuring out, but these are rare individuals.) Knowledge
about horses can be ours for the observing. We can watch the best
in the business and learn much this way. We can figure out a lot
for ourselves. If we're advised to use a draw-rein on a certain
horse, let's try to figure out why this would be a beneficial rig
to use, and then let's find out the correct way to use it. If we can
find no one to give us the answers, let's turn to the written word.

Sure, no book can substitute for personal experience. The old
horsemen who learned by "riding the XIT rough string" really
learned, and could afford to be scornful of book-learned horsemen. But a book can teach you *some* of the lessons of another
person's experience, and that can be a help. I know that when I
started I couldn't find much help anywhere, and could have gotten
a lot of mileage out of just a little bit!

So here it is—as much of my experience as a trainer as I can
put on paper. If it proves of some help to you, my struggle to
get it down in words will have been worth it.

Meridian Meadows   DAVE JONES
Tallahassee, Florida

Contents

1.

What to Look for in a Horse

I once worked for one of the top Quarter Horse men in the country. He produced winning horses. His conformation horses also performed and won working events where such events are extremely difficult to win—in California. When he was asked what he looked for in a top horse, he gave a one-word answer: "Conformation." He was right; if you have superior conformation, you have everything. You even have brains, for I've never seen a stupid horse that had a good head.

Styles come and go. The horse with superior conformation might not be the halter winner of the moment. But a good horse is a good horse. Conformation will prove out in the long run.

Let's start with the head. It should "go with the body," being just the right size to fit the rest of the horse. The forehead should be flat, with great width between the eyes; the latter should be large, brown and have an intelligent appearance. Personally, I don't like any white to show around the eye. Describing the overall expression and general appearance of the head, I would say, "calm and intelligent." Ears should be small and set well up on the head. No mule ears, please! Width between eyes and ears denotes brain room.

The muzzle should be small and the mouth should be narrow. A horse that wears a regular bit has a wide mouth. A narrow-mouthed horse uses a 4½-inch bit; a wide-mouthed horse uses bits 5 inches wide and up. A small, narrow muzzle is refined.

The little muzzle should swell to a muscular jaw. This is emphasized more in a stallion than in a mare. A stallion should have a *powerful* jaw.

The neck should be fairly long. It's almost impossible for a horse to flex properly a short, stubby neck. The throatlatch should be refined and neat. A neck "put on upside down" is undesirable. This condition is called a "ewe neck." Any horse with this type of neck will be high-headed and much more difficult to get to flex properly.

The gelding and mare should never have cresty, stallion-type necks. The stallion often gets more and more neck with the years until he appears to be "all neck." The gelding shouldn't appear too masculine, and the mare should definitely be feminine, with a neat, trim neck.

I like medium withers on a horse. The withers should be high enough to keep the saddle from slipping, but very high withers require a saddle with a special higher fork to allow clearance between fork and horse. The extremely low-withered horse is called "mutton-withered." This type of horse is to be avoided if possible, as the saddle will slip around too much unless the horse is almost cut in two with the cinch. This makes for many training problems, all of which are related to the extreme discomfort the horse must learn to live with.

I believe that the shoulder line influences head carriage. An extreme and long shoulder line is characteristic of the Arabian horse. He carries his head high, with a proud manner.

The working-type Quarter Horse often has a steeper shoulder line and the lower head carriage that goes with it. The shoulder line that is not as long is desirable in some types of working horses, and should be considered neither a blessing or a fault—it's a case of what you personally admire.

The girth of a horse is of considerable importance. A horse should "cinch up big." Heart and lung room explains this.

The underline is also very important to the working horse and means "depth through the loin." If a horse cuts steeply up from the cinch to the flank, he has little depth through the loin. Such horses look like a greyhound, which is all right in long-distance racehorses but extremely undesirable in any horse that works off his hind legs. Reining, cutting and rope horses should be deep through the loin.

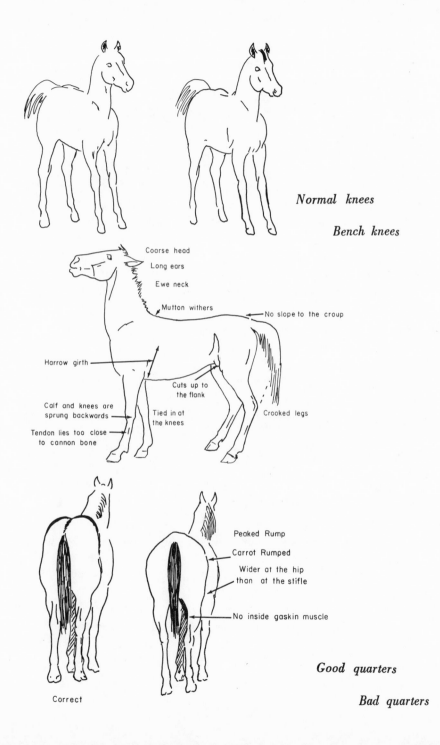

Normal knees

Bench knees

Coarse head

Long ears

Ewe neck

Mutton withers

No slope to the croup

Harrow girth

Cuts up to
the flank

Calf and knees are
sprung backwards

Tied in at
the knees

Crooked legs

Tendon lies too close
to cannon bone

Peaked Rump

Carrot Rumped

Wider at the hip
than at the stifle

No inside gaskin muscle

Good quarters

Bad quarters

Correct

I like quite a bit of slope to the croup, with the tail setting low between the buttocks. I don't like a prominent tail bone which stands up over the back like a pipe. There should be a cleft down the rump deep enough "to hold dust," which means that the horse is built to support powerful rump muscles. The slope to the croup allows the horse to get his hind legs well up under him when turning.

A horse should have good depth of hip—the length from the flank to the point of the butt. This means power in his propelling force, the hindquarters.

Hind legs should be in correct alignment and neither too straight nor too crooked, for infirmities are inherent with either fault. An imaginary line running along the back tendon from fetlock to hock should just touch the point of the butt. This holds true only if the horse's hooves are properly trimmed and he's standing straight. A long toe will make the horse appear crooked-legged. The hoof should have approximately the same angle as the pastern.

Bone should be adequate to support the horse's bulk. Don't buy a horse whose legs appear *too* refined. Very small bone spells trouble in the long run.

There should be a definite separation between cannon bone and tendon. You've heard horsemen say that a horse has "good flat bone." A horse has no flat bones in his legs. But when the tendon stands well out from the cannon bone, the appearance is sort of flat. The horse whose tendon lies close to the bone looks (and is) "tied in at the knees" in front, and appears too delicate behind.

The cannon bone should set under the knee in the front legs. This gives the horse a slightly knock-kneed appearance, but it's correct. Some horses' cannon bones are set too far out, giving a straight-legged appearance. This is a weakness called "bench knees" and is very bad.

When viewing the horse from the rear, greater width should be observed at the stifle than at the hips. This means power and ability to work off the hind legs. The gaskin muscle should be fairly even, and show almost as much on the inside as on the outside. A horse with no inside gaskin muscle will wear down his hooves on the outside, with the inside surface of the hoof building up while the outside is wearing away. Uneven gaskin muscling means hoof trouble or, at least, constant hoof attention.

The horse's toes should point straight ahead. Constant hoof trimming can often improve or correct crookedness, but he's a better colt if this isn't necessary. (Lower the outside of the hoof if he toes out; lower the inside if he toes in; results are instantly observed.) Toeing out is a worse fault than toeing in, and is harder to correct.

No discussion of conformation is complete without considering conformation under saddle.

The horse should appear alert but not jumpy. He should travel with his nose in—never out like a pointer dog. The neck should flex, giving a proud appearance. The tail should be carried gracefully, out from the butt. Sometimes a horse that one might overlook in the pasture will look brilliant under saddle.

Most important of all, the whole horse should always appear to fit together in correct proportion. Different breeds and types may vary somewhat in their special characteristics, but a good horse is a good horse, and if you're lucky enough to own one, learn to do right by him!

2.

Developing the Pleasure Horse

I couldn't begin to count the times I've been asked the question, "Where can I find a gentle, young, good-looking Western horse for my family?" There are plenty of average horses around, but the true pleasure horse is hard to find. Yet I believe that the gentle, well-adjusted pleasure horse is really the mainstay of any breed of horses. The really marketable horse today is the gentle horse that a beginner can hack around on in safety and yet not be ashamed to ride. No novice will stick with horses long enough to become proficient if his first horse jerks away and kicks at him with malice aforethought.

Horses are all so different that it is almost impossible to set up standards to insure that a gentle, well-behaved animal will be the result. I think, however, that those who breed and raise horses can take a big step toward the desired end result by following this formula:

The dam should be gentle. The spook will raise a spook. The sire should be a working horse that has proved to be a successful show horse. It is hard to show a silly horse and a pleasure to show a well-mannered one.

The kind, intelligent mother will care for her colt twenty-four hours a day. She will warn him about things to fear and instill confidence in him when he should be unafraid. If a man walks into the pasture and the mother flees in terror, the colt will have a fear of man instilled in him. If the colt sees his mother walk up to a man to be petted and have her back scratched, the colt will have little fear of the human.

The man should thoroughly acquaint himself with the colt dur-

A brand-new colt sure smells awful . . .

but he's mine, and I love him.

Don't go to sleep, Mama. We want you to play with us!

ing this pre-weaning period. If he can get the colt to come to him for feed and grooming, he is on the right track. The colt should be caught and led. If plenty of time is allowed for this, fighting will be kept to a minimum. The colt's confidence in the man will grow.

At weaning time, the colt's world explodes. The day the colt is taken from his mother is the worst day of his life. He is inconsolable. The human cannot help him except by leaving him alone. However, the old saying, "misery loves company" is very true; two or more colts should be kept together during weaning. They will do much better.

Soon after weaning, the colts should be separated from fillies to prevent early-maturing equines from accidental breeding. This is the time when colts learn to be buddies. They form friendships that are very strong. As with humans, this is a time for fighting, and buddies will stick together to fight other colts, sort of like the wild kids that roam the streets of the big cities looking for a

The kind, intelligent mother will care for her colt twenty-four hours a day.

"rumble." These little spats are natural with the horse and are a part of growing up.

However, this is a time when colts can also learn to be wild. Close association with the human is desirable at this point. In practice, most colts of this age are turned out to shift for themselves until ready to be broken. If time can be allotted to handle these younger colts, the result will be well worth the effort. They can be led, longed and even driven. Handling will pay off in making the colt a gentler horse.

But deviating *too* much from the normal situation is detrimental. The colt should grow up in a paddock or pasture with colts his own age to develop good horse-to-horse relationships. Raising the colt in a stall with humans as his only companions is an unhealthy way to raise a colt. If he is in a pasture and can play with his friends, he will be gentler with other horses. We have all seen boxstall-raised horses that wanted to kick every other horse in sight. The colt may get a few lumps and scratches from his buddies, but he will be much healthier mentally.

So, at this stage, the colt should have strong horse-to-horse and horse-to-man relationships.

This is a good time to watch for the "lone wolf." The colt that forms no friendships with the other colts needs a very strong horse-to-man relationship. For some reason, there is often a colt that is driven from the bunch and is forced to remain an outcast. He wants to belong but is not accepted by the crowd. Rather than leaving him to follow along at a distance—rather than leaving him always to be on guard against aggressive colts, turn him in with an old gelding that would relish the company of a colt.

When training time comes, the degree of gentleness, how he feels about humans, his past experiences, the gentle breeding and the considerate handling will all determine whether he will be a gentle, reliable pleasure horse or a "cowboy's" horse. There are only a few cowboys, but there are sure a lot of "green ones" who would like something that they can feel safe with.

Let us say that we have a good pleasure-horse prospect. The colt is gentle, is in good shape, but has not been kept in a box stall with sugar hand-fed to him to make him silly. He is just right to train. We must train him by going about it just right.

Colts need play and companionship. Here two young stallions romp together. A smell, a nip and then . . .

All training comes down to *punishment* and *reward*. By punishment, I do not mean getting wild-eyed, foaming at the mouth and flying at the horse with a club. Punishment means a sharp cut with a whip, calmly and immediately carried out as a result of the colt's bad manners or mistakes. Punishment is a harsh word or a gruff growl. Punishment is a rap with the lead rope when the horse is unruly. Punishment must be immediate or the horse cannot associate it with his wrong action. It should not be severe enough to terrorize the colt. It should not instill a long-remembered fear of the trainer because the colt should *have and show affection for the trainer, to become a pleasure horse.* Many people handling show stock horses will never know or comprehend this. It is a shame, for these people are missing a lot of the fun in this horse business.

"Reward" means a kind word, a mouthful of grain, a pat on the neck, loosening the cinch and airing his back, a rest or almost anything to show the colt that he has done a good job and that we were pleased with him. He will want to please his trainer. The trainer should let him know when he has.

Training should proceed in an orderly manner, one thing at a time. A good horse may result from hurried training, but chances of success are greatly increased if the proper time is allotted to each phase of the training.

. . . sparring begins. Around and around they go, nipping, striking and kicking.

This is wild play, but only play. As soon as one horse quits, they both quit and the game's over. Such play builds muscle, stamina and friendship. Of course, there's a limit. A few more months and these colts can never be turned out together again.

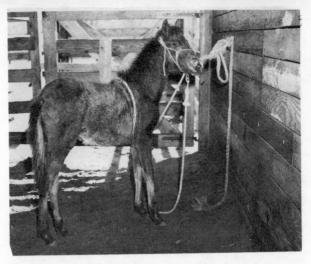

Young colts and fillies need a lot of handling to grow up into gentle, well mannered horses. This is Bruja, a Colombian Paso filly, at her first session of concentrated handling. She's tied to a strong ring set into a solid wall. The rope around her girth is a soft, heavy foot rope, tied with a bowline knot so it can't tighten on her or cinch up to make untying impossible. There's almost no way that she can injure herself.

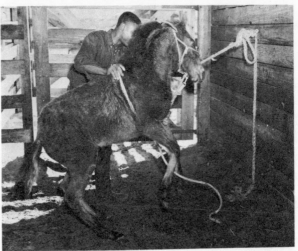

Bruja isn't very happy about this, but she must be handled. Jimmy Lee Thomas is petting her to get her used to the touch of his hands. Rigged this way, with the rope between her front legs and through the halter to the ring in the solid wall, she can't kink or break her neck and it's impossible for her to throw herself backwards. She'll soon give up.

Now she looks more peaceful, so her hooves are handled. They were trimmed when she was weaned. She was also hoof-branded for identification.

Ken Sirco leading Bruja. He's come to an understanding with her. Continued handling is important to keep them gentle.

All this takes a little patience. But if anyone asked what question I *most* often hear as a horse trainer, I would have to say it's this—"How long will it take?"

I get this question even from old boys who should know better, but I always get it. Of course, my answer is always in the form of a question. "What do you want the colt to do and how well should he do it?" But I still give them no real answer until I've handled the colt for a few weeks.

The more you handle horses, the more you should realize how little you know. A trainer who really wants to be good will learn something every day from his horses.

There are trainers who can have a colt really percolating in a month or two—the colt can "do it all." The novice horse-owner will be impressed by this cowboy—but the horses won't be. They'll be afraid.

I think most any trainer can knock and spur a good handle on a colt in thirty days. I can, but I won't. This colt has no place to go but downhill. A horse must want—or at least not be afraid —to work to be any good. Who in the world wants a horse he has to half kill to get him to work?

I can relate an example I'm not proud of. Quite a few years ago, a man came to see me about working a couple horses for him. He had to get them broke to sell, and they weren't the kind to be worth much either way. He was very persuasive and I agreed to do what I could in thirty days.

When I saw the horses, I wondered why he bothered. Neither was worth breaking and both were rank. One colt bucked hard every time he loped. I tried three rough methods to break him of this, and the third worked. I knocked a rein on him with a doubled latigo and the spurs.

The other colt would spook and run. I rode him hard and knocked a rein on him pronto.

I called the man after I had his horses two weeks and told him to come get them. When I rode both for him, he was tickled to death. He didn't see how I had done so much in two weeks. He said they were "broke to death." Of course I told him they had been handled rough, and then he told me those colts had thrown everybody in the county. They had been spoiled before I got them

The bowline is the most useful knot the horseman can know how to tie, because it never slips or tightens up. It is used to lead colts, to make a neck-rope, to tie up a hind foot, etc. Here is my version of how to tie it: Step 1. Hold rope in your hand, just as pictured above. Step 2. With first and second fingers, twist a loop in the rope until you have a duplicate of this photo. Step 3. Pull the end of the rope through the loop to gain some length to work with. Final step. Bring the end of the rope around the rope and through the loop. The completed knot can be left very loose and will not tighten. Other forms of the bowline will tighten as a horse kicks and struggles. Practice this knot until you have perfected it. You'll use it forever.

and I just knocked it out of them so a cowboy could ride them. Rough methods for rough horses.

However rough my methods were, they weren't nearly as rough as what is commonplace with many well-thought-of trainers today. There wasn't a spur mark on either of them. Sure, I had knocked on them some, but I never beat them up, never used a chain on them, never hit them with a club. I just paid back in kind when they dished it out.

A good horse must be trained slow and easy. If trained right, he'll retain what he learns and will always be a good horse. He'll be safe because he won't dread his rider. A horse shouldn't dread to be ridden. He should like it.

My point is this—sure, horses will work if trained by rough, rank methods. A cutting horse might make the top ten with some "tiger" always knocking on him. But most horses made this way are mediocre and are no pleasure to handle and be around. A horse will do a better job, work in the right manner, be a friend and stay working if he has been trained right. He'll enjoy working and will like his rider.

Remember, anybody can brainwash a horse. Not everyone can train one.

3.

Training the Western Colt

The start a colt gets has great influence on his future life. Take a gentle colt that's been used to nothing but love and kindness and put him in the hands of a club-and-chain trainer, and you're going to get a very spoiled colt as a result.

There are many trainers who make "cowboy" horses. These horses are never gentle. They're snorty, prone to buck and want nothing to do with a man. They respect a man but have no trust or affection for him. They might have a good "handle" on them, may work a cow, may become top rope horses, but they have no affection. I think most horses can work and still like a man.

How good a rider should a man be to attempt to start his own colt? I think he should know quite a bit about horses and gear and be able to figure how a colt's mind works. He shouldn't have to be able to ride a bucking horse.

PRELIMINARY TRAINING

Let's assume that the owner has raised the colt, or at least has owned him for some time, and that he and the colt are familiar with each other. The colt is fairly gentle, his feet can be picked up, he leads well and can be blanketed. Blanketing a colt really helps to get him used to being saddled.

The first few days are spent saddling and unsaddling the colt. I sack him out and continue to do this every day until the colt is fearless of waving and flopping objects. This is to prepare him for saddling and to get him used to the sudden movements close to him. He must learn to stand still and not jump away as his nature tells him to do.

An old feed sack is about as good a tool as one can use. Let the colt smell the sack, then start rubbing him with it. Soon the movements can be speeded up until the sack is flopped all over and around him. A few days of this and he should have no fear of the saddle.

Many colts will soon learn to stand for the sacking, but others need to be hobbled. There are many varieties of hobbles on the market. The soft-leather Utah hobble is a good one for this purpose. A fairly long, soft rope is tied to the hobbles so that the colt will learn not to run when hobbled. If he tries, the trainer should jerk him to his knees or jerk him clear down. Of course, the ground in the training pen should be soft and free of rocks when this is done.

If the colt continues to fight the front hobbles, a back leg should be hobbled and drawn up. (This "Scotch hobble" is discussed at some length later in the book.) When the colt is restrained in this fashion, he should soon gentle to the sacking-out process.

The first time a colt is saddled, the rig should be eased on and cinched up only tight enough to keep the saddle in place. He must stand still for this, so hobbles are in order here. I have a method of lowering the saddle on the colt that is actually neither easing nor flopping it on him. This is impossible to describe as it takes some real practice. Great care should be taken so that the off stirrup won't hit the colt on the elbow; the pain that accompanies this can easily make a colt hard to saddle. The trainer should practice saddling on a gentle horse before attempting to saddle a colt. (*Never* throw on the saddle, as we see some people do.)

The cinch is gradually drawn a little tighter each day until it's tight enough for riding. *The saddle should fit the colt.* A narrow saddle on a round-backed colt will have to be cinched so tight that there is danger of getting him "cinchy," or always dreading the cinch when it is drawn up. A colt will try to compensate for the tight cinch by "blowing himself up," which means that he takes a big breath and tenses his muscles. You'll think that the cinch is tight, but after going twenty feet the colt relaxes and the cinch is loose.

California hackamore, showing how reins (mecate) are tied up to lead or tie the colt.

The Colombian Paso mare Sarita Montiel models the California hackamore. This fiador is of mane hair, very light, to offer little hindrance to the action of the hackamore. The reins are tied on the bosal the same way they would normally be tied with no fiador. The fiador is up against the heel knot, where it should be.

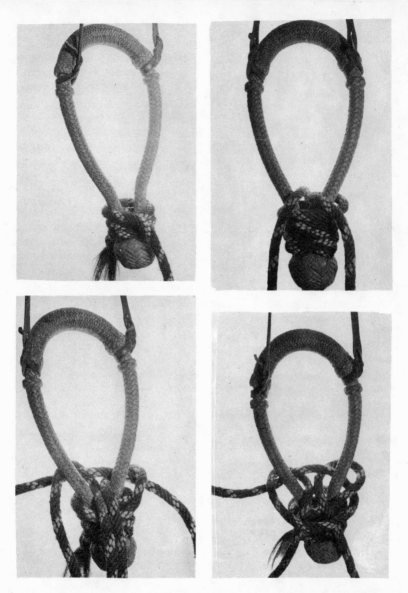

How to affix the mecate (reins) to the bosal to make the hackamore:
Step 1. *Take as many wraps with the mecate as are required to get the
desired fit.* Step 2. *Reins are formed. Since the reins are often put on and
removed from different sizes of bosals, they are called "falsareindas"
(false reins).* Step 3. *The reins are run through the bosal, and where they
run around the bosal sides, they are pushed down a few inches to form
loops. The end of the mecate is then run through, from right to left, to
form the chin knot and lead rope.* Step 4. *The knot is completed and ready
to use, though not pulled tight. Notice that there is only one wrap in front
of the reins. An old Californian once told me that if a man took more than
one wrap in front of his reins he didn't know his job.*

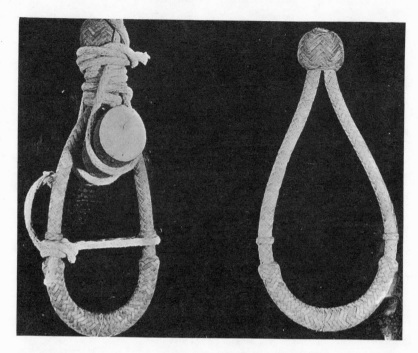

This is the way I shape a hackamore (it will not work on a hackamore with a cable core). The hackamore should be left to shape for a couple of months. Hackamores also shape with use; I have a great old hackamore with thirty years' shape in it that I wouldn't trade for most horses.

The big starting hackamore is then adjusted to the colt. This hackamore should be the California style, stiff, but shaped to the colt's head. It is good to use a *fiador* (throatlatch) at very early stages, though later the hackamore has a better action without it.

A word of caution here. When I say hackamore I mean hackamore, not a hackamore *bit* or a pressurizing noseband. I mean a good rawhide hackamore and rope reins or horsehair mecate (reins and lead). For the average colt a hackamore diameter of ⅝-inch is sufficient, and the inside length of the noseband should be about ten inches.

A new hackamore should never be put on a colt; it needs shaping first. I tie in the back of the hackamore where the first wraps of the mecate would go, then put a can or a piece of post where the horse's jaw would be and tie the can down tight. I then tie

This is Pasquero Grande (nicknamed Maxie), a young Andalusian stallion owned by Chandler Cowles, of Tallahassee, Florida. Maxie came to us to get a correct start. He was a little stronger and more afraid of man than the average horse of the same age, and was hard to get next to. He was impossible to sack out when hitched to the snubbing post, so he was thrown down. We broke him to hobbles when we let him up. He's hobbled in this picture. The rope attached to the hobbles is to jerk him to his knees if he attempts to jump while Ken rigs him to drive.

Driving. Note Maxie's calm manner.

Putting on long lines. By running the line through the hobbled stirrups the pull is kept low, which is correct when starting colts. Note the bit guard, which holds the bit up, off the mouth's delicate bars. This keeps the colt from getting his tongue over the bit and protects him from abuse from it.

Backing. The low pull makes it easy.

in the sides to correspond to the size of the horse's face and allow the whole outfit to shape as long as possible. Needless to say, it's wise to purchase the hackamore well in advance.

In use, the hackamore should be cleaned and saddle soaped frequently to prevent the rawhide braid from drying out and standing up. The rough rawhide can act like a rasp on the colt's jaw. If the colt has tender skin, the noseband and sides that come in contact with the jaw should be wrapped in soft cloth.

The reins should be tied to the saddle, short enough so that the colt can't get his head down to buck, but with enough slack for him to be able to tuck his nose in and relieve the pressure. A longe line is attached to the back of the hackamore. It can be tied to the fiador loops. The next step is longeing the colt on this line. This teaches the colt to carry the saddle without bucking, for if he tries, the hackamore instantly punishes his nose. He will learn to lope in circles and can be taught to stop and start in such a rig.

The value of *a whole lot* of longeing eludes me; a week of this is enough in most cases. It depends on how well the colt goes. If he fights or "sticks" at any phase of training, time should be taken to get the colt going well before proceeding to the next step.

Many people always longe their horses for five or ten minutes before getting on. I don't do this because I don't want the colt to feel he's got a permanent right to it. I want eventually to be able to saddle up, get right on and go to work.

The next progressive step is driving the colt in long reins. Many trainers don't like to do this. I think it helps any colt, so I always do it. If you want a gentle, well-trained colt, driving *always* helps.

When driving the colt, the stirrups are tied down (hobbled) under the colt and the long reins run through them so that the pull will be low. This gives control. Stirrups flopping around unnecessarily frighten the colt. The hackamore reins are tied to the horn as in longeing.

I use rope that I have taken apart and braided back in a simple pigtail braid for my long reins. (I buy a good Manila farm rope of half-inch diameter for this. Thirty-foot reins are adequate in most cases.) This makes a strong, fairly soft rein that won't get hard and kinky in damp weather.

Driving the gentle colt can be done by one man, and I prefer to do it by myself. An assistant can easily become tangled up if the colt jumps, turns and runs. But if you're alone, then a small, strong breaking pen is a *must*. A sixty-foot circle makes a nice size for starting colts. (If you have no pen and can't build one, then you will need an assistant to lead the colt in front of you until he understands what's expected of him.)

The colt might jump around when he first feels the long-lines around his hocks, but this little flurry soon passes. I start, stop and turn the colt both ways. If he backs willingly he can learn all about this the first lesson. If he appears reluctant to back, put it off until tomorrow. Keep on driving him until he backs straight and evenly. When he's working in fine shape and seems unconcerned about the whole thing, he's ready for a ride.

THE FIRST RIDE

This first ride won't be at all tough. The colt knows how to handle, which puts him way ahead of a colt that hasn't been driven. A man on his back is new, but since he knows control and is gentle, there's little to fear.

I like to take a little feed with me. The colt is saddled and the hackamore is rigged for riding. I give him a little bite of feed and stick my toe in the stirrup and start to ease on. If he gets excited, I step down and wait a while before starting up again. I hardly ever "cheek" a colt to get on (pulling the colt's head around to you by pulling the headstall or *fiador*). I want him to stand, and "cheeking" forces him to turn as you mount. Almost all colts will stand if you use patience. The fidgety kind can be held by an assistant, who must be sure not to stand directly in front of the colt.

The feed is really a help at this stage. If he's too scared to chew, *watch out;* you're way ahead of yourself. Slow up the training, drive him some more and add to the driving by putting a little weight in the stirrup a couple of times a session. Make no attempt to get on until the colt will stand for mounting in an unconcerned manner.

I suppose that everyone has a moment of nervousness when

Maxie initially fought the rider's mounting and dismounting, so much time was spent on this aspect of his training. By this time he was pretty good about it.

mounting a colt for his first ride. We all dread the unknown. But I have never been thrown from a colt on his first ride. (Don't go to the door; that pounding you hear is me knocking on wood.)

Sometimes the colt will spook and jump a little. This is perfectly natural. A pat on the neck and some soothing words will help him over this hurdle. I try to get him to take feed from my hand when I'm in the saddle. When the colt accepts the rider without undue fright, that's about enough for the first mounting. It's very good if the colt is moved, gently turned both ways, and started and stopped a few times. I think that the trainer is way ahead not to get on and off too much this first time. Use good judgment and quit while you're ahead.

The colt can learn more the next ride. Trotting can be attempted. Tap the colt on the rump with your hand and squeeze with your legs at the same time. The colt will learn to move forward by leg pressure in a few rides. How forcefully the leg pressure is applied, coupled with the general way the colt is handled, will determine his speed.

LEG AIDS

From the colt's first couple of rides, we'll go on teaching leg aids. When turning to the right (clockwise) we'll press in at the cinch with the left leg and keep the right leg away from him and vice versa, counter-clockwise. In a couple of weeks the colt will turn a little on leg aids alone. We'll use leg aids all through hackamore training.

The squeeze will also be used. I suppose almost everyone squeezes with the legs to move the horse ahead. Ahead to what is the question.

Start using the squeeze to leg the horse up into the bridle or hackamore.

If we squeeze and let the reins alone, the horse will move off. If we squeeze and hold back with the reins (very lightly), we're "collecting" the horse. We're telling him that we are going to go into a collected gait—or a stop—or a back-up. Legs tell him to get ready. Reins, body weight and the use of individual legs aids tell him what to do.

Early in the colt's training, we should grip the colt and rise up slightly in the stirrups to signal the stop. Two weeks of this and the colt should be very light. Of course, no steady pull should ever be used with a hackamore, but the colt is starting to collect himself, nevertheless.

When practicing the roll-back, we signal the stop, then couple a leg aid with the ordinary use of the reins. Since the colt generally takes the correct lead out of a roll-back, we'll be teaching him to take a lead with leg pressure when we do this.

We'll also squeeze when we want to back up. Aids go like this: At a lope we'll signal for a stop. Colt slides in and stops. Leg pressure is released. Then we stand, squeeze in time with his backward steps. Couple this with light pulls on the reins, also in time with his steps.

Maxie at a walk. Again, note his relaxed manner.

The canter or lope. Note the wide loose rein. The snaffle bit is handled much as a hackamore would be. Ken is using a wide rein, taking up and giving out slack. The horse is uncollected, as he should be for the first months of his training.

The stop in one movement. Colt is loped along the fence. Rein is pulled on the side toward the fence as we will stop, dwell, then turn into the fence and jump out. Note how far the colt has his hind legs up under him. Rider is off the seat, weight on the stirrups and spurs having a light contact.

None of this training should be hurried. The colt will gradually learn to rely more and more on leg aids. Spurs have a tendency to annoy, so they should be used lightly and as a signal, never as a punishment. The horse should thoroughly understand leg aids and work them correctly before spurs are ever applied.

I sometimes carry a bat or crop but don't use it excessively. When the bat is applied with leg aids, the horse will wake up and work. Taps with a bat coupled with leg pressure often get good results.

When the colt responds and does something right, he should be rewarded. This will speed up training fifty percent or more. Give him a bite of something he likes when he does the right thing and growl at him and/or whack him with the bat when he fouls up. Some horses are fools and become nippy when fed from the hand. These are few and far between. The trainer must always use judgment, but the practice of rewarding the right moves shouldn't be abandoned because we once had a horse who bit people, looking for a tidbit. A horse should never be fed from the hand except when he's working and the feeding takes the form of a reward.

We must sometimes drill a colt to the point where he becomes sulky and ready to fight. This is a great time, just as soon as he gives the first inkling of doing something right, to give him a tidbit, a minute's rest and a pat on the neck. This will often keep a colt from becoming "mad" clear through and will save weeks of training. The colt's thoughts might be something like this—"I was sure ready to splatter him, but what the heck, he's not such a bad guy after all."

If the colt doesn't relax, however, or even if he comes out one day feeling a little rank, you're going to have to know how to control him. Getting good control with a hackamore is the most misunderstood part of hackamore training. Let me emphasize the fact that you need no wire on the noseband. Neither do you need any sort of "controller" to work on the nerves of the chin. These gimmicks have no part in hackamore training. They can only cause a messed-up colt.

THE DOUBLE

Control means the "double." The double is often misunderstood because it's hard to explain. So pay particular attention to this:

When the colt spooks, wants to jump, run or buck, the double is instantly applied: *One* hackamore rein is pulled, hard and abruptly, to force the colt around in his tracks. This should be done in the training ring, as it is much easier to double the colt toward a fence than it is out in the pasture. The fence keeps him moving forward and cuts the work in half.

The pull must be sudden and hard enough to accomplish a full turnaround. If you ride with steady pressure on the reins, it will be almost impossible to double the colt. You *must* double from a loose rein. If you've misjudged and not pulled hard enough, slack off, allow the colt to run on a few steps and try it again, this time with more force.

Keep the colt in the small pen until he's been doubled a few times and understands this control. If you try doubling in the pasture or large pen with the colt running wide open, you'll pull him off his feet, and the result will be a hard and dangerous fall.

The double teaches the colt to be responsive to the "tuck," which is pulling back on one rein to slow down or stop. If the colt refuses to heed the tuck, the double should immediately be applied.

The results of the double are drastic. The colt learns to dread it. The colt should generally only be doubled when using the hackamore. If he must be doubled with the snaffle bit, adequate precautions should be employed to insure safety to the colt's mouth. Safeguards consist of leather guards, coupled with a snug noseband, to keep the snaffle rings from being pulled through the mouth.

Since drastic results are accomplished from doubling, the temptation is always with us to double too much, for every little misdemeanor. *The colt can be spoiled from too much doubling.* Doubling must be done to teach control and should only be used to correct a bad mistake such as bucking, running too fast and refusing to tuck down to a slower speed. Use the double sparingly.

THE TUCK

The tuck is simply what the name implies. It is used to make the colt tuck in his chin toward his chest. When pulling down from a lope to a trot, one rein is used; the pull is low and not too forceful, and is a pull and slack. If the colt pops his nose up instead of giving to the tuck, the nose is quickly pulled down by the other rein. It's correct to use one rein and then the other. It's *never* correct to pull both hackamore reins at the same time. A colt will shoot his nose up immediately if this is done. The tuck teaches the colt to arch his neck and is very important in hackamore training. How the colt's head is set in the hackamore affects his whole future as a reining horse. It should be done correctly.

In circling the colt, the rein should be pulled with the hand

Tucking the colt to develop a head-set.

way out to the side, no higher than the saddle horn. The method is to *pull and release,* with the pulls only as hard as necessary. The colt will "bull" his head (set his head against the pull) if a steady pull is used. The few that won't "bull" against you will become "limber-necked," which means that you can pull their heads right around while they run straight ahead. Leg aids should be used, coupled with correct hackamore handling.

Never ride the colt in a pasture until you're sure you have him under complete control. The colt might spook and run. The natural tendency for the novice is to take a hard steady pull on the rein, and this means big trouble. Establish your control in the training pen and try to remember the correct way to double if a bad situation comes up. The double works in the pasture as well as in the arena as long as the rider doesn't freeze.

The good hackamore man realizes that getting the colt's nose hard or insensitive is to be avoided. He raises and lowers the noseband every half-hour. The weight of the bosal will, in time, deaden the nose. He uses different hackamores. The colt is generally started in a fairly heavy, stiff bosal. (The *bosal* is the nose-

When starting colts, the wide low rein, pulled and released, should be used. Illustrated is the wide low rein.

band—the hackamore is the whole rig. Another definition is that anything over a half-inch in diameter is a hackamore, less than a half-inch is a bosal. "Bosal" and "jaquima" [ah-kee-mah] both mean "noseband" in Spanish.) Then he switches to a lighter, stiff one. When adequate control is achieved, he may be ridden in a heavy, limber bosal. or what he goes best in.

Most people should alternate the hackamore with the colt bit. A light bosal is first used *with* a colt bit, the bit being used more and more until the colt is safe to ride alone in the bit. When he starts poking his nose out, go back to the hackamore. If either nose or mouth starts getting insensitive, switch to the other gear.

Some colts work the hackamore far better than the snaffle bit— and vice versa. It's silly to work a natural snaffle-bit horse in the hackamore. If he's far superior in one rig, keep him in it.

 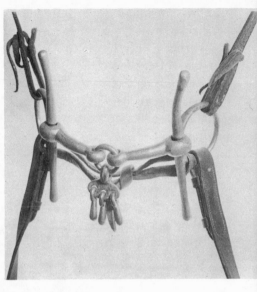

(Left) : *A starting hackamore—very stiff and heavy. It's too much hacka-more for a light-nosed colt, but works fine on some we get. The sides are an inch thick.*

(Right) : *A colt mouthing bit. When first bitting the colt, such a rig is proper. The colt plays with the "jinglebobs" and starts in early to make mouth moisture. The long metal cheeks keep the bit from jamming in the colt's mouth. The chin strap also helps.*

The constant drill of making a hackamore horse should be alle-viated with rides in the pasture and some cow work, if possible. A colt generally loves to amble through pasture and woods. We work in the training pen for a while, then go to the pasture to relax the colt. Not too long. Don't tire him out.

Cow work teaches the colt that there's a reason for learning fast stops and roll-backs. Almost all colts will *look* at a cow, and will speed up their work while cowing. A colt should never run wide-open in starting gear (hackamore or colt bit) unless he's heading a cow or rating up on a calf for roping.

Always ride to the head when crowding a cow. Riding to the

rear may result in a bad fall. The colt will head a cow and turn her back. Head the cow again—always to the head. Hold the cow in a corner and head the cow when she tries to break out. Be alert and the colt will be alert.

When the colt has been ridden from six months to two years in starting gear, he will be put into the finishing bit, usually some variety of curb. This can be accomplished by riding him in the small-diameter bosal under the bridle, and gradually using the bit more and more until the colt is straight up in the bridle.

The horse-owner can get into all sorts of trouble when training his colt, however, and going to the curb bit too soon is probably the single biggest colt spoiler. People rush too much, believing that they should accomplish something new every day. A colt needs time to have his good habits firmly implanted in his mind. He learns nothing unless an orderly training schedule is followed.

The straight curb bit (with no provision for a double rein) should never be used with a direct pull; only with the neck rein. As I feel that neck-reining with no direct pull is *never* a good thing, I'm not too much in favor of the straight curb bit. The method I prefer is to use some form of Pelham, riding the colt with this type of bridle at home, then going to straight curb at shows to conform to the rules. I'll go into this in more detail in Chapter 5.

4.

Leads and Cues

Years ago, when I was a fledgling trainer, "leads" was a word foreign to the lingo of a horse trainer. If I had told a buddy that his horse was in the wrong lead, he'd have thought I'd lost my marbles.

We never paid much attention when a colt missed a lead unless he was constantly in the wrong lead. We would then work the colt more in the direction of his bad lead. If he didn't take a right lead, we would force him into it by whirling him onto his lead and then making him work it until his right was as good as his left. This was not a common occurrence. It seemed that when leads were less important, we had less trouble with them.

When we had a horse with poor leads, we said "he ain't handy to the right." If he got his front leads and did not change his back leads, we often said "he ran out behind."

The situation is different now. Everyone's an expert on leads. If I work a colt while his owner observes, and the colt misses a lead, watch out. I'll sure hear about it. The colt may spin, slide, run backward and be so light I can tie a thread to the reins, but let him miss a lead and, *oh boy!*

Sometimes when I work a colt before people it seems as though the only thing they watch for is a missed lead. I can work the colt through all sorts of maneuvers and will draw no comment, but miss a lead and it sounds like the Metropolitan Opera chorus all singing, "Hey, he missed a lead."

So, since leads are so important, I now concentrate on them and, to get a horse completely foolproof on leads, I use what might be termed "elementary dressage." The way to have surefire lead control is to control it yourself. Dressage training produces instant and obedient response to the rider's commands, which are issued by hands and legs by collection. So we must strive for collection and obedience.

Naturally the colt isn't born with an understanding of collection. He must be patiently taught this. The difference between reining a collected horse and a horse behind the bridle is smoothness. The horse that isn't up in the bridle must wait for rein signals that are always a surprise. When the signal comes, the head generally flies up. The uncollected stop is a high-headed, bouncy thing, figure eights are jerky, changes of lead are haphazard.

Your colt should already know a lot about leg aids and mild collection from his earlier training. Now you've got to build on that knowledge. But remember, Rome wasn't built in a day, and never was a horse trained in a day either. Collection is a long-time thing, and so is the responsiveness to collection.

Work for the most part should be accomplished in a training arena. The work period should go something like this:

Walk, trot and lope for about ten minutes to loosen the colt up and work out any stiffness that might be the result of previous schooling. Then devote ten or fifteen minutes to work that the colt already knows fairly well. This might be a collected lope starting in a large circle and working in smaller and tighter, then out to a large circle and a stop, both directions.

If the colt fouls up on any old stuff, that should be straightened out. If all goes well, something new may be tried, such as rolling back on the correct lead. Care should be taken not to overwork. If the colt seems unable to grasp a new idea, it's better put off for another day than to keep the colt in collection too long.

Work should be ended with an easy walk around the pasture without collection. This gives the colt a chance to "unbend," cool out and relax. Then the colt can be turned out in a pen to roll before cleaning him up and putting him away.

The result of using leg aids to signal and collect the horse will be a fine stop that the colt will keep. He'll be so responsive to directional signals that we can signal whatever lead we want by applying leg pressure. He'll back up straight and fast. He'll work with his chin in and neck arched, this posture being necessary for lightness in the bridle. He'll retain his good mouth as he always works lightly in response to reins and legs. He can easily learn a maneuver such as the side pass, since he responds lightly to legs and bridle. When fully trained he should be able to take a lead going straight away at our desire.

A few examples of how to apply leg aids while working might be in order. First, let's correct a common fault. The colt is one-sided. He'll take a left lead and work it every time. He will never take a right lead under saddle. We'll now make him take a right lead.

Take the reins in the right hand and the bat in the left. Walk the colt along the arena fence with the fence on his right, and stop him about four feet out from the fence. Turn him into the fence and hit him hard enough with the bat to jump him into a run. A very abrupt turn to the right such as this makes it impossible for the colt to take the wrong lead. Leg pressure should be applied with the left leg on this right turn.

The fence forces the colt to turn 180 degrees to the right. The next step is to keep the colt in the right lead. This is best done by circling. While using intermittent leg pressure, lope the colt in a right circle, gradually reducing the size of the circle. This work on the correct lead, but the unusued lead, will make the colt use unused muscles—like making a right-handed carpenter pound spikes with his left hand. The colt (or the carpenter) will get stiff and sore, so work should be light in the beginning. This exercise should be a daily thing, but the use of the bat can be minimized when the colt learns to come around handily. He can be given more of this as his muscles harden.

The time will come when the colt will work equally well with each lead. To keep him this way, we must give each lead equal time when working. Circling is a fine exercise. Every horse should be circled every day, clockwise and counter-clockwise. The colt should be started from a walk or standstill into the correct lead on varying sized circles. Another part of daily drill should be the roll-back on the fence such as we did to force the colt into his unused lead. Roll-back and go into a circle. Leg aids should always be applied, using the pressure on the opposite side from the desired lead. I think the aid should be applied lightly, on and

Here the Colombian stallion Relicario spins in correct position. He's spinning left (note foretop) and is turned slightly into the direction he's going. I'm giving him a slight leg pressure with my right leg.

off, rather than a steady leg pressure, which would be tiring to rider and horse.

The colt will become completely used to leg aids. If he becomes "dead" to them and refuses to respond, tap him with a bat near the spot where leg pressure is applied. This is much better than applying more force or resorting to spurs.

Most colts will become responsive enough to take the correct lead when leg pressure is applied. We should be able to stop the colt, start him into a lope going straight away on either lead we desire. This is our goal.

The flying change of leads is more difficult to accomplish. While circling the colt one way, we signal by leg aid and reins that we want to change directions of the circle. In a figure eight, the change of leads should occur in the exact middle of the eight. Many colts do this handily, especially if the figure eight is executed at a fairly fast lope. Others seem to find it difficult to the point of impossibility. We should train for it like this:

Circle the colt four or five times one way, then stop. From the stop, swing the colt abruptly into circling in the other direction. Practice this daily until the colt is very handy. Of course, the correct leg aids are applied.

Start the colt the same as before. Circle four or five times, then switch leg aids and pull the colt into the other circle. Try to time this correctly. Apply the leg aid when the colt's hooves start to leave the ground. The right time to do this will feel natural to you. It will be very smooth.

But sometimes the colt bobbles, misses his leads and finally ends up by being correct in front and in the wrong lead behind. He is circling "disunited."

When this happens, keep the colt circling in tighter and tighter, but don't force the lope. The colt will realize that the way he's traveling is very awkward, and will want to drop into a trot. As soon as he trots, apply a forceful leg aid and lope him in his circle. This will be on the correct lead as he'll leg into it naturally.

Practice this in both directions. Start the figure eight clockwise one time and counter-clockwise the next time. Don't overdo it. If the colt has been suppled enough and is responsive to leg aids, he'll soon be switching his lead at the right time as long as we time the maneuver and the leg aid correctly. We shouldn't ask him to switch when he's unable to. He can't accomplish the impossible.

For the occasional horse that just can't grasp the figure eight and the change of lead, we must find a place to work that is not quite level. Since it is harder to maintain balance on uneven ground, he'll be forced to change.

To keep the horse working well, don't work a standard figure eight. Unfortunately, it's always very easy to teach a horse some-thing he shouldn't do. If we practice figure eights quite a bit, the colt will start to anticipate the change of leads and will switch a couple strides before he should, making a jerky, uneven figure eight. So we should circle a couple times and cross over, then circle about five times the other way before crossing back. By always varying the number of circles, we'll stay ahead of the colt and make the change of leads impossible for him to anticipate.

SPURS

Spurs are a necessary evil. They are evil only because most riders do not know how to use them. Spurs should never be used with enough force to leave a mark.

Many trainers feel that the colt should really be hit hard with he spurs—then they should be used sparingly. It works this way. The colt is made to fear spurs and will jump away from them. But he will gradually get over his fright and his apprehension and this hard force must be used over and over again. This is a "hurry-up" form of training. It is forcing a colt to do something before he has learned how.

Spurs should be used to enforce leg aids. It's easier for the horse to feel spurs than the leg. The natural time to start using spurs is when the horse gets a bit sluggish and does not respond to leg aids as alertly as he should. The spur should be applied easily to emphasize the leg aid. The rider should couple whip and spur rather than really hitting the horse hard with his spurs. There is no excuse for hard spurring. It will ruin a handling horse.

In most cases, spurs should not be used in front of the cinch. The old saying on a good cow outfit was, "Back of the cinch belongs to the cowboy, front of the cinch belongs to the outfit."

If the rider has enough self-control to just *touch* a horse with the spurs in front of the cinch, this can be a definite aid to a roll-back or spin on some horses. However, using the spur just back of the cinch will suffice for most horses.

The primary thing the trainer must remember is to get the horse trained. What works for one horse will need to be varied for another horse. The trainer must keep an open mind and be ready to try different gear and methods on his horses. One colt will work a snaffle bit but will not hackamore. Another will hackamore but will be hard in a snaffle. One colt will dread a bat but will work fine for spurs. Spurs will agitate some colts and a bat will agitate others. Some colts need neither. The trainer needs a supple mind. He must find the rig the colt works best in, change around if the colt hardens and becomes insensitive. Use all gear and training aids with discretion, and then teach the horse's owner how to work the colt.

5.

Getting and Keeping that Good Rein

Much training advice starts off by saying, "First, get a good rein on the horse."

What is a good rein? There are probably as many answers to that as there are horsemen. I'd say that a horse with a good rein would work lightly with a flexible neck and a tucked chin. He should maneuver easily, work off of his rear end, back readily and turn as well one way as the other.

Some horses won't take a good rein. Others must be batted around to keep them sharp, and the man that says "tain't so" hasn't ridden a lot of horses. Some horses break out light and stay light. We can't judge them all by either the reining champion or the deadhead.

The colts that I'm allowed plenty of time with will generally come into neck-reining so gradually and easily that neither the horse nor I can actually realize when we stop plow-reining and start neck-reining.

This is maybe due to the fact that the hackamore colt is started with the wide rein (hands held way out to the side and down low). He is turned by pulls and releases, never a steady pull or the colt will learn to bull into the hackamore and take his head away from us. The pulls are as light or as heavy as necessary to accomplish their purpose.

When the colt learns the meaning of a very light pull coupled with body English, we take in the reins—meaning, we don't hold our hands as far out or as low down, although the hand should be about as low as the horse's withers.

As we work the colt with the hands in close, we apply the neck

The squaw rein.

rein while also pulling him. This is called the "squaw rein." Soon the horse will be working with the neck rein and body English, and we have a "reined horse."

Sometimes we have to break a horse that just does not have it in him to work light and easy and we have to get a little rough to make him work at all. We give him all the chances but he just will not come to us. He is a dog or a deadhead, and we have to work him accordingly. He may wake up and be valuable as a using horse.

I bat this horse around with a doubled piece of latigo. When I lay a rein on the horse's neck and he "dogs it off," I bat him alongside the rein, and he does turn. A few sessions of this and he will neck-rein going slowly.

It will probably take a combination of the popper, squaw rein and maybe even draw reins to get this deadhead doing figure eights, but he must do it, for the horse that will not lope along in figure eights and circles won't do much of anything else either. These maneuvers teach the change of leads and general hardi-

The squaw rein in action.

ness, and they should be done a lot. They also keep the horse light as he isn't running in a straight line, which can soon turn him into a runaway.

He will probably come along well after we stir him up a little with the popper. Let us carry it with us so we can keep him going well. Such a horse may develop into something, so we will try to do the best we can by him. It's a lot easier to break and train a good one than it is a plug, but we do the horse a service by making him into something. We may keep him from becoming fox feed.

Don't forget the draw rein here. If the horse goes to bulling or running off, refusing to heed bat, rein or anything else, bring out

A regular draw rein. With draw reins it's possible to double a horse that's almost impossible to double any other way. You can force a horse to work in such a rig. Leverage does it. The bit guard makes mouth injury impossible.

Colt backing in draw reins. This is very good, for the pull is low. It's easy for a colt to back if his head is low, almost impossible if he's "star-gazing." Notice that Ken has his weight off the seat, which allows the horse to back fast and straight.

the draw rein and rig it on your snaffle. You can turn the horse with this. A few sharp doubles and he's paying attention again.

If we make no mistakes with our colt, he'll probably be working well when we first put him in the finishing bit. He'll go along all right for a while, but chances are he'll go sour in the curb bit. His head will come up; he'll throw his head and get heavy in the mouth.

For one thing, we've been using an easy rig on the colt—hackamore, or snaffle, and then into the curb. But now we get heavy-handed just when we put the severe bit on the horse. He gets worse and worse and soon he's like the horse that never had a good start.

Many people get excited when working cattle or roping. The hands go up and they pull too heavily and steadily. Many will put a tie-down on the horse when he goes sour. I won't say that this is wrong, but there are other ways. It seems a shame to waste all that careful training that we've put into this colt.

If we have only a slight tendency to have high hands but handle the reins all right otherwise, we can use a running martingale to keep the reins lower.

I sometimes put the horse back in the starting rig. Draw reins have a place here. Where a curb bit may make the head go up, draw reins help the head go down. Use the old snaffle with draw reins and you will have a lot of leverage without injuring the horse. A few sessions and he'll be working as before. This horse already knows how to work; he is just soured in the curb bit.

After we take off the hackamore and put the horse in the bridle, we change styles. We neck-rein instead of plow-rein. The pull is necessarily more steady in the bit, whereas we rely on the pulls and releases with the starting rigs. But put the hackamore or snaffle back on the horse and we'll be surprised at the lightness that he's lost. Actually, the horse has not gone downhill as much as we might think. He has changed his mode of operation as we have changed our method of signaling.

Draw reins can be used when neck-reining and we can also plow-rein if we have to. We can wake him up by doubling him. We must conscientiously work to improve his rein. We forgot to rein just right when roping, working cattle or just riding, so the fault is ours as much as the horse's.

The head-set draw rein. This rig is best handled with an indirect rein (neck-rein) or a "squaw rein" (one rein used indirectly and one rein used directly).

Cutting horses and some rope horses often stay in the hackamore. These horses are self-workers and get very little reining from the rider, so naturally they have less chance of going hard.

Changing the rig often helps. A change of curb bits (curb to snaffle) often helps to lighten up the horse. A neck rope may be of use. I make mine by tying knots in a piece of old lariat rope. I then drape it in front of the saddle and rein and stop the horse with it. It often helps in keeping a reined horse spinning and is sometimes even called a "spinning rig."

I've run through most of the usual problems that are encountered once the colt has started working in his finishing bit, but as with all phases of horse training, what works with one horse may not work with another. We have to try everything and see what helps the most.

A trainer who is interested in getting the best work out of his horse should always wonder if he's handling him properly and if he's using the correct gear. He should periodically examine his methods and equipment. It's ridiculous to use the same old gear and methods of our ancestors if there is a better way, *and usually there is*.

I've been training since 1943, have done so all over the country, used different methods, and have come to the conclusion that I know very little about training and am not much of a horseman. However, I intend to keep right on trying to find better methods and equipment.

All equipment has its faults and its good points. Hackamores are both good and bad, as are snaffle bits. The old California bits are very good in design but are generally used incorrectly. The English Pelham and Weymouth have a poor design but are often used in an extremely skillful fashion.

The Californian knows that a bit should be loose-jawed, contain a pacifier (a cricket that makes a noise when a horse rolls it with his tongue), have a lot of copper in the mouth (copper has a very pleasing taste to the horse) and be designed to hang and balance perfectly. These are good bits.

The flaw is the way they are used. The California bit must be used indirectly—the neck rein. No provision is made to use a double rein. The colt must be hackamored and/or snaffle-bitted right to the finishing stage of his training.

I certainly don't want to knock California methods. This art, developed on the West Coast, produces results unknown elsewhere in the world. They have made it a science. The California reining horse works the closest to perfection of any horse that is neck-reined. But it is impossible to get perfect suppleness and lightness when neck-reining the horse.

The neck rein, no matter how expertly applied, in time teaches the horse some bad habits. The head is pulled too high when the rider slides his horse. The indirect rein pulls the horse a bit out of position when circling or figure-eighting. The horse must re-

(Left): *A colt bit with a bit guard of my own invention. The beauty of this rig is that it keeps the bit off the tongue and bars, if this is desired. By buckling it tight over the nose, the bit can be raised in the mouth; when the colt learns about the bit, it can be lowered. The rings of the bit can't be pulled into the mouth. This rig is used mainly with draw reins.*

(Right): *A soft rubber-mouth Pelham—a very useful bit to use between the rubber colt bit and a regular Pelham. A light touch on the curb rein will help to bring the colt's chin in.*

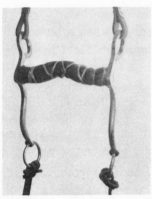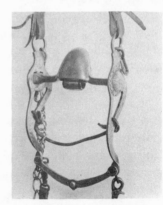

(Left): *A common way to rig a cutting horse curb bit. The cutting horse must be jerked back quite often in early training without much reinsmanship involved. So, the bit is padded with rubber to soften the jerk on the mouth.*

(Right): *This bit falls between the spade and the grazing bit, is called the Salinas in my terminology. The principle is that of the spade, though results don't compare; this is a hurry-up version. Almost any horse will take it and like it.*

spond to the directional signal of the neck rein, but he also responds to the pull of the rein *directly*, and this forces him to work a bit out of position.

The Californian, by beautiful hand position, pulls the head only a *shade* out of position. He says that the horse's body should be straight when turning, spinning or rolling back. But his horse isn't straight; the head is pulled a slight bit *away* from the way the horse is turning. In truth, the head should be pulled slightly *into* the horse's turn.

The California methods are less than perfect, but the rest of the country is mediocre. Head position is very bad away from the West Coast. Many trainers do a fine job when working the colt in snaffle bit or hackamore. They all fall short of the Californians when using the indirect rein. Their methods and bits are not as good. I speak here only about the reining horse when being neck-reined. This is not said derisively—it is a condition that needs some improvement and we must study the cause and effect.

We need the neck rein but place too much importance on it. How a horse neck-reins isn't as important as his manner of work. If the horse is supple, responsive and works without falling out of position, he is a true reining horse whether he is ridden under a stock saddle, in full spade or under an English saddle with two bits and four reins. We tell ourselves that we have good reining horses. "It ain't necessarily so."

The horse is a creature of habit. He learns both good and bad habits. Men, too, are creatures of habit. We learn to ride and handle reins a certain way and never seem to improve. A trainer of thirty years' experience will handle the reins the same way he did as a boy. If all his horses stop with their noses up in the air, he'll say that this is the way a horse should stop. He'll say that a horse doesn't stop right when his nose is in and his neck is arched.

We all know the old saw that "low hands make a low head." This is true. We often resort to the running martingale to get the pull lower. When the neck rein is used the hand must usually be high, or all give-and-take with the horse's mouth is gone. Only a top reinsman can keep his hands low, the heel of his hand staying on the withers, arm crooked to allow his hand to stay in front of

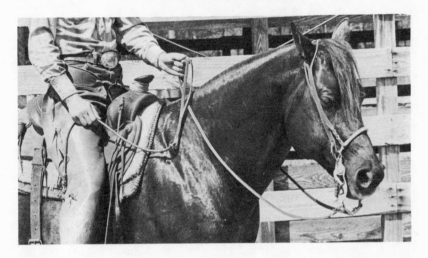

Salinas bit with a bosal to keep the horse's mouth shut. Note hand position. Reins come from the bottom of the hand, which allows the rider to get his hand much lower than if they came from the top of his hand.

the fork of the saddle. This is the absolute lowest that a reinsman can keep his hand. The only give-and-take is by pulling in or letting out the reins via the romal, or reins held in his right hand. This is a major give-and-take, but minor ones are needed to give the horse's natural head movements some nature of freedom as he lopes. The finishing bit makes good reinsmanship bad.

Why not keep the colt in the hackamore or snaffle bit? Is the finishing bit needed?

In general, the colt gets hard in the hackamore and snaffle bit. He learns to "Scotch" after a few years. His work suffers. The trainer will switch bits and bosals to lighten him up, but each new rig will work for only a short time. The proper time to switch to the finishing bit is when the colt's working his best. The curb will help keep him light.

I realize that I've been criticizing without offering a definite solution. I have criticized English bits, California methods and the whole country in general. All right, then, here it comes.

My first solution to the reining problem is to *not* neck-rein all the time. Be ye not afraid to pull your horse into position! We can and do use Pelhams and Weymouths and lightly pull the

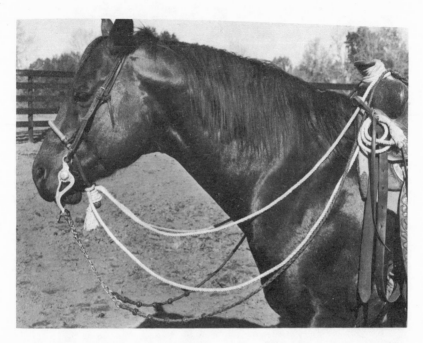

This is the Californian's double bridle. The small bosal might be compared to the snaffle bit. The bridle is used more and more, eventually being used alone without the bosal, though a small bosal is still often used without reins, like an English cavesson, to keep the horse's mouth shut.

horse. We can use leg aids to further signal our intent to the horse.

There isn't much give-and-take of the reins when neck-reining a horse. You must start with a tight rein if you want to slide your horse, as you have no place to go with your hands. The horn and your body restrict a straight-back pull. Your hands must go up to get the reins tight enough to stop the horse, so the head must go up too. The Californian's solution to this is to take up the slack by pulling on the romal with the right hand, letting the reins slip through the left. This is a far better system than raising the rein hand so high, but it's almost impossible to use the hand delicately when performing quick maneuvers. Strong-arm stuff prevails.

A better way (at-home practice) is to ride with double reins, two reins in each hand. With a hand on each side of the horn,

Ken Sirco lopes Steel Helmet in a circle. Note that the horse is correctly bent into the circle. He's on his left lead.

slack can be taken up and the hands can be kept low. The stop, roll-backs, circles and figure eights can be practiced with a correct hand position, and the horse can learn to maneuver in correct form with his head down and neck arched. Of course, these methods can't be used at a show, but this is no real reason for not riding the horse the right way at home. If you foul up the horse at a show, correct him at home. Leg aids can be a big help with a reining horse, for in time the horse will learn to work from the legs so well that you can get by at a show without getting on his head too much.

There are a few western bits on the market that make provision

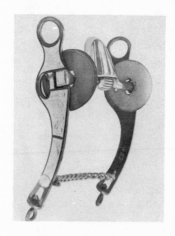

(Left): *The Santa Barbara spade, probably the best bit in the world for the reining horse* if the rider understands its use. *The balance of the bit is perfect—the horse* must *carry his head at the correct angle for the bit to be comfortable. The main drawback is that double reins are almost impossible to use with this bit. The four-rein method is to use a light bosal when teaching the colt to carry this bit.*

(Right): *This bit has been put together for me by the Carroll Saddle Co. It's named for me. The features are a copper-covered port with a barrel cricket, loose-jawed, and a provision for double rein. Altogether I think it's a very nice bit.*

(Left): *Dave Jones bit on Steel Helmet. Note the guards to keep the bit from pinching the lips. The cavesson keeps the mouth shut just as a light bosal would.*

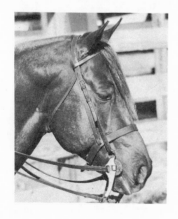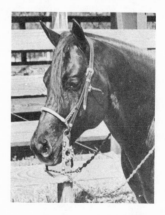

The Santa Barbara spade with a bosal to keep the mouth shut. Notice the hang of this bit.

for the double rein. With them, the double rein may be used at home and the top rein can be removed when showing the horse. These bits are one solution, but unfortunately they don't have all the provisions I previously mentioned as being required for a good bit. Mass production doesn't make for a good bit because the length of the sidebar and the width of the mouthpiece should be taken into consideration for each individual horse. A training stable should have at least four different bits to get a good fit on a particular horse. One mouthpiece might be 4¼ inches wide, another a full 5 inches wide. One sidebar might be 5 inches long (and work fine with most horses), but another horse might work better with a 6¼-inch sidebar.

I'm currently having some bits made by the Carroll Saddle Company in Tubac, Arizona. We are trying "this" mouthpiece with "that" sidebar, and using sidebars made with a slot for the top Pelham rein. All these bits have copper and a pacifier (cricket) in the mouthpiece; they are loose-jawed and balanced correctly. These bits work much better than any I've previously tried. My opinion is reinforced! A good California bit can be made better by providing a slot for double reins.

The cricket and copper seem to be universally Spanish. On a recent trip to Colombia, I was told about the importance Colombians place on a horse's mouthing the bit and making mouth moisture. A horse that never works the bit has a "dead mouth." He soon pokes his nose out, and his head gets higher and higher. The horse working the bit flexes his neck, bringing the chin in, which leads to the horse giving his head to the rider's hands. This is vitally important! The Spanish word for the horse's act of working the bit, making mouth moisture, is *tascar*, doing it is called *tascando*.

Many horsemen, through their dislike of anything Spanish, I guess, hate to see a horse work a bit. I have heard people discuss this as a fault. "That horse works all right, but he chews the bit. Guess I'll have to tie his mouth shut with baling wire." Oh, boy!

Many a good reining horse would continue to work instead of "sticking" (rearing on roll-backs, balking, taking the wrong leads, etc.) if he had a pacifier in his mouth to relieve some of the tension. But the people who own such a horse would ridicule the idea of using a Spanish bit. "If he sticks, I'll take a club to him."

A cutting horse man once told me something that personifies the idea that I'm against. This guy was riding a good colt and was using a very expensive, "in vogue" cutting horse saddle. But his hackamore was a mess. It consisted of an old piece of lariat for a noseband, wrapped with baling wire. The reins were braided from a discarded foot rope. I asked him why the heck he didn't get a good hackamore and a decent mecate (reins).

Says he, "I would, but it'd look too much like California."

6.

Training the Rope Horse

First things come first, so the first thing with a rope horse is to break him out right. He ought to be going pretty well and reining very well before we go to our first calf. Of course, we have also roped off him a fair bit to accustom him to the whine of the rope and we have pulled objects up to him, such as blocks of wood, weeds and branches.

Okay. Let's start rating calves. If this is to be just a ranch rope horse, this will be the most important thing he can learn.

We'll arm ourselves with a bat and go out to the cattle. Let's pick a calf out of the bunch, preferably a slow one to start with, and follow him around, behind him, just the distance we like to rope; our correct rating position. We'll bat the horse up if he is too far behind, and pull him in if he gets too close, until we are staying just where we want to be.

When that calf gets tired, we'll go after another one. Horses like to play with cattle like this, but don't overdo it and tire the colt.

When rating is down pat, rope a calf. Catch a good calf around the neck and gradually stop the horse. If there's a helper, let him remove the rope and stay on the colt.

I like to dally-rope at this stage of the game, especially if I have to work by myself. If something goes wrong, I can drop the rope and not spoil my horse by getting him all tangled up and rope-burned.

Let's say that I am by myself. I follow the calf until he starts to tire, then I rope him. I keep the horse going until I ride up close and dally. My horn is wrapped so I take two dallies, get off

Here's how cow work starts. The horse is Pal, a Quarter Horse stallion owned by Hugh Royer, of Columbus, Georgia. Pal's a young horse, too young to have much cutting or rope work poured into him, but a taste of it will get him primed for things to come. Pal had never been roped off of before the day this photo was taken. I got him used to the rope, then loped behind the calf and "laid it on." (I'm squalling something to the colt, but don't remember what it was all about.)

and hold the end of the rope so the dallies won't hop. I also have my horse as I am dallied up close. The calf is a little tired and not too rank to start with, so he doesn't fight me and scare the colt back.

I stick my hand into the loop, release my hold on the end of the rope. The rope comes off the horn, and I keep hold of the loop, which opens up and releases the calf. If I had been tied on, chances are I would have had to leg down the calf and tie it to get my rope back.

I will now ride the colt around a little and make sure he is gentled down. He has been rewarded for doing a good job on the calf, and we are very friendly with each other. We will now go catch another calf and go through the same thing. Then we call it a day.

I enjoy dally-roping so I keep doing so quite a while. If the horse's path bends toward the rodeo arena, I will have to start tying the rope to the horn and tying down the calf.

The adantage of "dar la vuelta" (dally roping) is obvious here. I can dally up short on the calf. I can also turn the rope loose if I "get in a storm." This isn't the right time to get down and tie the calf, but I must release it.

If that's the case, I tie the rope hard and fast, make sure I am packing a sharp knife and go rope a calf. I equip the horse with a back-up rope, so I will be able to keep him from following me up to the calf.

The back-up rope is a piece of clothesline that runs from the bit to a pulley on my fork and ends up looped in my belt. It is a little longer than the lariat. This backs up the colt after I get off and go to my calf.

Some guys (rough and tough ones) just slap the horse in the face and scare him back. I think that the horse should understand his part in helping up-dump the calf, so the back-up rope is my way of doing business. The horse soon understands that when I go after a calf, he is to back up and keep that rope tight. If you've ever tried to leg-down a calf with a horse that comes up and gives you a slack rope, you know as well as anyone how important the tight rope is. Keep the back-up rope rigged until the horse flies back and does it every time. If you have to use your green colt at a contest, use the back-up line in the arena. It would be better to keep the colt out of contests as long as possible, as

This gentle calf makes things easy. I ride up, dally short, reach down and turn the calf loose from the saddle. Pal thinks it's great fun. (The calf thinks it's just a pain in the neck.)

Some gentle calves are necessary for the training of a green colt. This calf is paddling along so slowly that I can heel it off a novice horse with no header helping.

excitement does a lot to foul up the colt. He will be good for a long time if we take plenty of time getting him going.

The roper's box can make or break you. You might have a great rope horse, but if he goes crazy in the box, you're out of luck. He should willingly enter the box, stand there collected, break out fast (when we want him to), run well to the calf, rate the calf perfectly, stop hard to bust the calf and work the rope perfectly when we're off and away from him.

The box is often the undoing of us all. To get the horse to go in and stand there when he knows that he will soon come out running as fast as he can, is something that takes coolness and brains in both the horse and the roper.

We can start out by getting the horse to like the box. Feed him in it. Groom him in it. Feeding and grooming him in the box will make him want to go into the box. Ride in and out of the box. Ride in, unloosen the cinch and air the horse's back there. Do all you can to make him want to go in the box.

Now, we want to get the horse to stand in the box without breaking out on his own when the chute bangs open. To do this, let's get him used to the chute banging open. He hears the noise and it's like a starting gun. If the calf freezes in the chute, the horse goes out anyway.

We'll bang that chute open while we feed him, groom him and air his back. We'll sit on him and bang that chute and still keep him in the box. Soon we'll have him where the chute banging open doesn't bother him too much.

Same way with calves. We'll release some and never go out of the box after them. We'll keep this up for a long time. Rope one, release one, rope two, release one. This is necessary, for if the horse comes right out after the calf, he would break the barrier at shows where the calves are given a long score.

Patience, patience, and more patience! When the horse starts doing something wrong, correct it! It'll take quite a while before we can hit the line just right to shave off the fraction of a second that might give us the winning time. We have to rope many calves before we have a rope horse and many more before we have a rodeo horse. We may never have one that will put us in the pay line.

Look, Ma, I caught 'im!

We should always pad the rope horse's back pretty heavily, as the calf creates quite a shock when he hits the end of the rope. If the back cinch isn't tight, the saddle will rise up in back and the horse will come up to relieve the pressure on his withers, thus fouling up the calf tier-upper. If the horse drags the calf while the roper is endeavoring to make the tie, loosen the flank cinch and the horse should stop overworking.

There's a lot of controversy about tie-downs. Some folks wouldn't use one anytime, anywhere. I don't think any calf ropers feel this way because if their horse needs a tiedown, they put one on him. It's pretty hard always to hold your reins right with all the speed and excitement of calf roping. We can't blame the roper for this, so when that head starts shooting way up on the stop, put on that tiedown. It's not a question of ethics but dollars. A horse does run freer and works better without a tiedown. The man who really trains his horse to stop without getting off on the reins has the problem pretty well whipped.

Now, some horses just don't seem to want to stop without the rein. Here's how to see if they will.

I like to work the very green colt on easy calves; not small, just

After roping a calf around the neck I dally, step off and release the calf from the ground. Left hand is in the loop, the dallies are jerked loose with the right hand and the calf is loose. Pal's trying to get his nose away from all this action.

not too rank. After I have roped quite a few calves and the horse has some idea of stopping after the calf is looped, I slap the horse on the neck to get his attention, then bail off. The horse should then stop and work the rope. The colt will generally catch on pretty fast when he's learning and interested. He'll start stopping better the faster I get down. It's best to get down during the jerk. When we graduate to ranker calves, the whole process should go smoother.

When we hear of nine- and ten-second times in calf roping, we can generally figure that the calves are easy. This is all right once in a while in a contest, but it doesn't help teach the horse too much. Big, rank calves are the thing for good rope work.

In the spring, when we want to ready up for the roping year, we may be forced to get little calves. If we do, we'll be disappointed in our rope horse when we get in an arena with rank calves. Here's the difference.

We come out after a little calf and throatlatch him. We bail off, the calf is busted, we go under the rope, flank the calf down as he's getting up and throw on the wraps and the "hooey" (two wraps and a half-hitch). All the horse has done is stop and back

The camera makes fast action look posed in this photo. The calf has just been released and the rope is still in the air. Pal's getting used to this kind of stuff.

"*Wow—what a smelly calf!!!*"

Here Pal enjoys a piece of range cube that we've had especially formulated for horses. It's a reward for work well done.

up, which is about all he ever has to do if he really "powders" the calf. But, if we get a bad run, a zig-zag calf or snag a bundle of really rank cowhide, we're in a storm. If we don't get a good "bust" on the calf, he may wrap up the horse in the rope.

We can give the horse a little rope-work/play by catching the calf in a place in the arena where the horse can't bust him or we can acquire a few really rank calves to rope at home. This is a good precaution to keep the horse working the rope with his eye on the calf.

In this day of ultra-fast roping, many ropers carry only one rope. I always carry two as sometimes a dollar can be made with the second loop.

I tie this second rope with three wraps of good string around a small D-ring tied onto my fork. This rig has not come down for me yet, but when I want it, the small D cuts the string when I pull.

I use a second loop at home, often on purpose, to keep the

horse used to that dragging first rope. When a miss is made with the first loop, I get my leg and fender over it, yank the second loop and fly after that calf.

When we rope a lot of fast, straightaway calves, the horse may get used to blasting out wide open and refuse to follow a turning calf. If we can't get turning calves to play with, we can always get a few goats. Too much goat-roping spoils the horse, as he will scotch (slow down) waiting for the goat to turn; a little of this is all right, though it depends a lot on the horse. If the horse is prone to scotch, he can't be slowed up much without really spoiling him, but a smart, rank goat will sometimes help the horse and also sharpen up the roper's eye.

I believe all good ropers are patient men. They have to be or there would be few good rope horses. A rope horse (a really good one) is hard to make, and not all horses can make the grade. Coolness in the box, terrific sprint, hard stop, cow sense and the agility of a mountain goat are requirements for a rope horse. And keeping a horse good requires real savvy.

7.

Choosing and Training
the Cutting Horse

Most admirers of the Western stock horse have seen cutting horses work in the arena. Many have ridden cutting horses and a few have trained them. When you see a horse really duck and dodge while heading a cow, you can bet that that horse has much natural ability and has had many hours in the practice arena with a top trainer on board. A cutting horse must enjoy cow work. He also needs practice and experience so he will make the right move at the right time.

The Western horse has a lot of heritage as a stock horse and I believe that the ability to work cattle is somewhat inherited. This is easy to find out about our own horses. If, in the normal course of working cattle, the horse makes a few good moves on his own with his eye on the cow, we have something that can be developed.

There are exceptions to this and one would be that the colt has been spoiled. If the colt has fear of his rider or has had his mouth yanked and hauled on, he'll have his head up and won't be able to see anything lower than an eagle. Everyday handling and proper breaking also affects the green horse just started. Trainers have different methods of training. Sometimes one trainer has difficulty settling down a colt, when another trainer might be successful.

A cutting horse must have the ability to turn fast, with his head low. Pivoting on the hindquarters is essential. A horse that turns on the front end won't be able to hold rank cattle.

A top cutting horse in action: King of Clubs is buckling down to work a very rank calf that is trying to come through him. A glance at this picture gives the reader an idea of the terrific action that goes along with cutting horses.

A cutting horse takes a terrific pounding through the years, so he should have the bone and back to take it. A horse with poor legs just can't stand the gaff. Good withers are another requisite. No matter how tight you cinch up, if the horse is mutton-withered and round-backed, the saddle will shift when cutting cattle. I am not saying that a round-backed, mutton-withered horse will not make a cutting horse, only that he would be a better one with good withers.

So, we want a well-built, intelligent horse that likes to put a cow in her place. If we have such an animal, the battle is half over.

STARTING THE COLT

It seems to me that one thing we especially must avoid is making the colt afraid of his head. Many trainers advocate the

Steel Helmet turning on to block a determined heifer.

snaffle bit and some colts work best in it. I like the hackamore for most colts and I'll be as gentle with it as possible.

I sometimes saddle the colt in his stall, put the hackamore on him and let him do some of his own head positioning. I don't tie the head too tight but allow enough slack so that he can flex his neck, tuck in his chin and take the pressure off the nose.

The next step is to get the colt going easily, and this means *take your time.* I generally drive the colt enough to teach him to start, stop, turn and back, as discussed earlier. I like to ride in a small pen so the colt has no place to go and can't run wide open. Just ride around the pen and try to get the colt to relax. If you move the colt, turn both ways, get him stopped and get off, you have made a good first ride. Keep him in the small pen until he is relaxed and will move around with his tail carried freely, not tucked up tight. He should be handling a little and stopping for you to get off before you graduate to a larger pen.

The hackamore rein should never be pulled on steadily. To turn the colt, the hand is held way out so he can see it, and he is turned with easy pulls and releases. You are then taking the colt's

*In the beginning there's much pulling and hauling the horse around.
He hasn't much of an idea as to what to do.*

*Much training advice starts with—"Get a good rein on the horse first."
Here a good rein is demonstrated. The colt is spinning around to head
the cow. However, his movement, while basically correct, is much too
slow.*

head. He does not know just when you are going to pull him, so he cannot prepare for it and set his neck against you. Just one ride using a steady pull will take many rides to correct, so we should allow no one to ride the colt unless he has good hands and understands the correct principles of handling the hackamore.

Should the colt want to buck or run, double him. The double is the "brakes" when hackamoring a colt. The colt responds to a light pull, straight back with one rein, or he gets doubled. He soon respects the double and acts accordingly.

STARTING ON CATTLE

If the colt is going pretty well and is strong, a little association with the cow would be in order. General cow work, roundup, herd-holding, penning, etc. would do him a lot of good. It's my contention that a young horse should learn how to do many things. He should help his rider open gates by siding up to them, and a little knowledge of the rope is never amiss. General cow work and handiness at an early stage is good for any colt.

So, let's say our prospective cutting horse is handy, switches leads easily and can stop and roll-back all right. We now have a colt ready to start on cattle. Of course, any outline of training is only a guide, since every colt will be different. For instance, one colt might respond to the shifting of body weight and neck-rein so easily and naturally that we always neck-rein him after the first month or two of training. Another colt might go out of position and foul up if we speed him up too much. But he might make the best horse in the long run, if given more time.

We need a fairly good-sized pen and some cattle that aren't too rank. Follow one gentle cow around and hold her in a corner. Then let the colt see what he has done. He's forced the cow into a corner and he's holding her there. At this point, the colt should be rewarded with a tidbit of some kind that he likes or, at least, with a friendly pat and a kind word. We must put across the point that we're pleased with him.

If all this goes well, perhaps we can give the colt a little more work. If the cow isn't too rank or fast, let her go down the fence a little, then get ahead of her and turn her back. Though at this

When starting on cattle we start with one cow in a pen with the horse. The horse blocks the cow on the fence, always working head to head with the cow. Pal turns the calf back with a hard block.

point we're doing a little following, then actually blocking the cow when we pick her off the fence. This can give the colt a lasting impression of how to take the cow off the fence, and also teach him not to fear the fence while still working slowly with a gentle cow.

After a few passes the cow will generally stop. She isn't able

This photo shows Pal coming around after the cow with the hackamore reins loose. He has learned to stop the cow in a period of only a few minutes. Such work is more like play for a colt, if it isn't overdone.

to go anywhere so she gives up. Let the colt stand facing the cow, reward him and then slowly ride away or dismount to signify that the work is over. If we had continued to work this played-out cow, the colt would have been forced to go up very close to get any movement out of her. This would lead to a couple of bad results. The colt might get the idea that he should always work right on the cow, which could lead to charging, and working so close can also give the cow leverage to slip past the colt. We don't want to lose cattle if we can avoid it, as a colt is easily discouraged.

Let's digress a bit and discuss charging. A horse generally charges to get more action from the cow. He wants to work and work fast, so he'll work up close to speed her up, bite or strike her. This kind of horse hasn't learned to stop and wait for the cow to bring the action to him, and has been hurried too much or spoiled in his training. We must be careful of this if we do much roping off our cutting prospect, for the cutting horse should block and fall back, whereas the rope horse should follow the cow. If we have a colt that won't do both, let's stop either the roping or the

The horse performs roll-backs on the fence when he passes a cow and turns her back. Here Pal is simulating a roll-back as he blocks and turns a calf.

cutting. There is no use having a halfway horse, one that is neither a good rope nor a good cutting horse. Seldom will one horse do both successfully.

Now, let's cut out a few cattle. We'll take the colt into the herd as easily as possible. We won't get technical or try anything tricky now; we pick out a cow who looks as if she will come out easily. After she's out, we let her go down the arena, and then reward the colt. We follow her out about forty feet. If she looks as if she might come back, we'll hold up the colt and block her if possible.

Steel is holding this calf in the corner. It's not doing anything, so neither is he. However, note how ready he is to counter any move the calf might make—front legs wide, ears forward, eyeballing the cow. He's ready.

Now, if this cow is rank, it's the time to get off and fool around with the colt, letting her get back in the herd. There's no sense getting the colt beaten by the first cow he's cut out. But if you have taken out an easy cow, in all probability she will just amble across the pen and stand. If this is the case, we'll leave her alone and cut out a couple more. If the colt gets the idea of stopping and waiting for the cattle to come back, he has done very well. We'll implant the idea in his mind that after he takes the cow out a little way from the herd, he should stop and block the cow's return.

This now requires daily practice. The colt shouldn't be shown too many cattle at any one time—his interest may fade as he gets tired. How many weeks or months will this need to be practiced? It depends largely on how much interest and ability the colt shows. When the colt can cut out cattle without spooking the herd, when

Cranky from working sour cattle, Steel is biting this calf. This is a bad habit, not only because it's hard on cattle but because a horse always gets out of position when he nips a cow.

he can stop, wait and block the cow's return, it is time to bring in help in the form of a turnback rider.

The turnback rider does not have to be a good cutting horseman mounted on a good cutting horse, though it sure helps. Still, you can get along with a pretty sorry rider and horse as long as the rider has an idea of what you want and will follow your instructions.

When the cow is cut from the herd, she should be allowed to move out well into the arena before the turnback acts. He then tries (quietly) to put the cow back with the cows she just left. The rider on the colt can direct the turnback as to when to move in and when not to. An overzealous turnback man can foul you up with a green colt. As a general rule, the cutting horse should not move forward after he initially follows the cow out from the herd. He should just block, duck and dodge and fall back to keep in working position.

It takes a little sense on the turnback's part to keep the cattle fresh and working as long as possible. He should fall back after bringing the cow to the cutting horse in order to give himself leverage and room to maneuver. If he is right on top of the cow, the cutting horse will duck the cow past him; he'll lose the cow and have to go down the pen to get her and bring her back. This is a surefire way to sour cows and to get them to running. Running cows are sour cows, as they'll just run from one side of the pen to the other between the two horses—and nothing will be accomplished besides sweating up the horses. Good help will keep cattle fresh and working much longer than will sorry help.

So, let's say we have a good turnback and our colt is coming along all right. Work might go something like this:

Cow-cutter rides in back of the herd and around until he finds the animal he wants. Herd-holder holds the herd and/or rolls it by the cutter to help him make his selection. Cow is cut out and eased from the herd. Cow trots out and the cow-cutter follows her for about forty feet and stops to wait for the cow. Turnback brings back the cow, and she ducks and runs a few feet to get by the cutting horse that is right there, *head to head*. Cow sees she cannot get by, so she turns back down the pen. Turnback has fallen back maybe twenty feet so he's in position to block the cow and return her to the cutting horse, and another head-to-head block is made.

When cow gives up her attempt to regain the herd, the cutter dismounts or puts his hand on the horse's neck, backs up and turns away, which allows the cow to re-enter the herd. This gives pretty fair play, and both cow and horse are getting good work. The cow finds that she can get back to the herd, and the colt, by being stopped from working, has won the play.

Even if one cow is a good worker and helps the horse learn a lot, don't just work the same cow over and over. Cut out different cattle, work them right, and they'll work longer. Almost all cattle will finally sour for you, and there is little you can do to freshen them. A really doggy cow will just stand after she has been cut out, and this makes both the cutting and the turnback horses work too tight to the cow. This teaches the colt to work too close, and he will lose rank cattle. A running cow is sour; when a cow learns to run, the colt must also run to get with her. Then they all need to

Sitting pretty. A good horse working a rank calf.

be reined. It does not take long for a good-feeling colt to decide that the working pen is a racetrack.

Once in a while we'll get a colt that really needs waking up. He'll lose cattle because he won't jump out and move, even though he is physically able and knows how to go about it. Such a colt needs some persuasion so we'll use whip, spur or both. (Of course, you can't use a bat in a cutting contest, but you should not train your horse at shows anyway; this is better done at home.)

The colt will eventually become accustomed to spurs so we'll use them sparingly, along with the bat. We want spurs to be a sig-

A man who knows stallions will savvy this picture of a stud mentally snaking mares into his band. Steel Helmet has just been cutting cattle and is walking by a few mares in a lot. Immediately, his head goes down, ears flatten into his head and his nose curls into a mean leer. He's telling those mares that they'd better go where he wants them to or he'll sure put them there in a hurry! (This horse is unusual in that he'll go into the "boss-hoss" act with a rider aboard him.)

nal, not a punishment; too much spur will turn the colt into a tail-wringer or worse. A light touch with the spur coupled with a whack with the bat will teach him to jump out or go right in to pick a cow off the fence. Keep after him with the bat when you aren't at the shows, and he'll stay much more responsive to the spur.

Don't continually peck at the colt with spur or bat, and leave him alone when he is doing all right. If we consistently reward him when he makes the right moves as well as punish him when he makes the wrong ones, it's easy to figure which he'll want to do. A reward can be a kind word or a friendly pat, as well as a piece of sugar. I have ridden colts that would become crestfallen at a harsh word. They would also show recognition of a friendly word after completing a nice head-to-head block. We don't have to fall all over their necks to show our appreciation.

There is a close bond between a good cutting-horse man and his horse. If the rider just sits in the saddle and hangs on, he is doing nothing to help the colt. The rider should look at the chosen cow and lean his weight the way the colt should go, but he should ride straight up. The shifting of the weight is slight, not the overdone, sloppy job we often see. The colt is aided more by the *idea* of shifting weight than by two hundred pounds flopping all over his back.

If we ride in a lackadaisical manner, all slouched back, behind the horse every jump and maintaining our seat by means of a death grip on the horn, the horse will do a sloppy job. We aren't eager and helping. The horse won't be eager either. If we don't *enjoy* cutting cattle, we can't train cutting horses. We must *know* that the horse will work right and then he *will* work right. The good cutting-horse man will make an average horse look good, while a sorry rider will make his horse lose cattle and will do a poor job in general.

8.

Understanding the
Cutting Horse Rules

The man who has only a vague idea of how a cutting horse works should thoroughly acquaint himself with the rules before attempting to train a cutting horse. A copy of the rules may be obtained from the National Cutting Horse Association. If you are serious about cutting horses, you should join the association.

Let's examine the rules and talk about them. These rules are the basis for judging all National Cutting Horse Association shows:

Rule 1.   A horse will be given credit for his ability to enter the herd of cattle and bring one out with very little disturbance to the herd or to the one brought out. If he (or the rider) creates unnecessary disturbance throughout his working period, he will be penalized.

A horse must have training, sense and a close mental sympathy with his rider to enter a herd quietly. The horse steps cautiously into the herd, pausing if the cattle start to mill around nervously. The rider picks the cow to be cut out and signals the horse. After reining a time or two, the horse should know which cow his rider wants.

The rider needs much self-discipline for this. If he is the nervous type, he must put it aside and concentrate on the job at hand. If he is calm and cool and alert, chances are his horse will be too.

I talk to my horses a lot, and they know what "whoa" and

Ken Sirco up on Steel Helmet. Ken's a novice cutting-horse rider. This was one of his first rides on a good horse. Here Ken gets in back of the herd to bring the cow out (Rule 1).

"easy" mean. I can tell my horse "easy" and we will go into the herd. A little leg pressure and a touch of the rein indicates which cow I want. We ease the cow out and try to block easily and casually when the cow turns to re-enter the herd. The real play starts when the cow is far enough out for the turnback man to start working.

In a contest, the contestant judges his stock and tries to select a cow that will offer good play for the horse. If he has to take the first one he comes to because his horse will not work the herd, he will always cut "traveling" cows that want to run instead of trying to get back to the herd. These cows come out easily but show bad.

The way in which you cut out the selected animal is important. Cows should not be "chipped" from the herd. To chip one out, the rider would cut from the front, with his horse facing the back fence. He'd have to take, off the end, one that wanted to come out. In all probability, this cow would be a runner or a rank cow, one that would either run from fence to fence showing no play to build points, or be so crazy that she'd lower her head and come through the horse to regain the herd.

Correct cutting procedure is carried out from the *back* of the herd. Whether you ride in from the corner or split the herd from the middle depends upon the number of cattle in the herd. When cutting from more than seven or eight cows, the herd should be split. It is always easier to cut from a small bunch than a large bunch, where the one you want tries to get lost in the crowd.

The speed of the horse in the herd must be correct for the type cattle you are working. This is another instance where close communion between horse and rider is necessary. Slow, herd-loving cattle require a decisive cut, smartly executed. Rank, spooky cattle call for a careful cut. Moving too slowly and cautiously can actually keep a cutter from making a cut, and he can be hung up in a tight herd for most of his working time.

The cutter should move to the back fence and signal to his horse which cow is desired by reining a couple times. The horse should then see the cow and bring her out at the necessary speed. The cow should be driven well out on the first cut to show the horse can drive cattle. The next cut need not be driven so deep. If any "chipping" of cattle is done, it should be the last cow, to insure that you are working stock when time is called. Being caught in the herd when time is called is not a disaster, but most cutters feel that it is better to be out and working.

The herd-holders will hold up the herd or move traveling cows past the cutter to allow him to pick out the cow of his choice. Most times the cattle will mill around when the cutter is in the herd. It is up to the herd-holders to contain the cattle. However, a horse moving too fast will spook cattle and make the herd-holders' task almost impossible.

At home, with only one rider to hold herd and turnback, he will hold herd, move the herd past the cutter for the cut and then fall back to act as turnback when a cow has been cut out.

Rule 2.   *When an animal is cut from the herd, it must be taken toward the center of the arena. If it goes down the arena fence, that is all right, but the horse should never get ahead of the animal and duck it back toward the herd to get more play, but should let the turnback man turn it back to him.*

When we first start our colt working cattle, we'll follow a cow, hold it in a corner and duck it back, as we are trying to get the

Ken's driving his cut from the herd. Styles in cutting change. Many years ago, a horse had to be exactly head to head and just blocked the cattle; the turnback horse did the work of setting up the cow. The current style is better, more like actual ranch cutting. The cow horse should block his own cow, getting a bit out in front to block the cow's run. Steel had blocked and is running to pass the cow and block her again. If the horse didn't stop a cow from running in actual ranch work, they could run head to head clear across a pasture (Rule 2).

colt to look at a cow. The colt, when learning to look at a cow, will push a doggy one with his nose, nip at her and do other things we have no use for in a contest. His life work will be cow work, and he must learn all about the animal. Going past a cow and ducking her back off the fence teaches the colt to go in by the fence and pick off the cow. He needs plenty of this so that later in his career he will not be afraid to get right in when a cow is on the fence. Picking a cow off the fence is done all the time when working cattle on the range.

But once we start using a turnback, we'll discontinue this practice. From this point on we follow contest rules. We bring the cow out, stop and wait for the turnback to bring the cow back to us, and seldom deviate from this. Cow-cutting is, in part, watchful waiting on the part of both horse and rider.

Rule 3.   A horse will be permitted 2 points each time the back
fence is used for turn-back purposes, etc.

If the cow gets far enough and deep enough to reach the back
fence, the horse has missed a block or two and has almost lost
the cow into the herd. Of course, a rider training a colt at home
often uses the back fence with no special thought about it being
either good or bad. But as the colt progresses into a finished
cowhorse he should gradually make better and quicker moves,
the back fence being used less and less.

Back-fence stops are sometimes caused by over-zealous turnback men who keep pushing a rank cow back to the cutter. It is
often better to get off a rank cow and be penalized for a "hot
quit" than to stay with her until she bulls through, for such a
situation often ends up as a back-fence stop, or a complete
five-point loss.

Rule 4.   If a horse runs into, scatters the herd, lanes or circles
the herd against the arena fence, while trying to herd an
animal, he will be penalized heavily.

This rule is often broken, especially with young, inexperienced
horses. The situation is generally something like this:

The cow comes back to the herd fast and shoots by or through
the cutting horse. He makes an attempt to head her, and in his
wild try to get where he is supposed to be, runs right into the
herd and scatters the cows.

Or the cow outducks the cutting horse and gets by him. He
overworks in an effort to head and loses the cow into the herd.
It is only natural for him to want to get to his cow, even if the
others do happen to be in the way.

A colt that is a little slow with his stops and turns will generally lose the broken-field-runner kind of cow. He heads her and
she ducks by before he can set himself, jump and start to head
her again.

We cut a cow from the herd and she leaves like an express
train. The cow bounces off the turnback man and comes back like
a rocket. The horse is between her and the herd. If he blocks her,
she will hit him and go on through. This cow makes a bad show
as very few horses have the ability to stop her. A really brilliant

This picture shows the terrific action that is a part of cutting cattle. Ken's left foot would be in the dirt if he hadn't pulled it alongside the horse. Steel is in the act of throwing himself to the left for his block. The very long rein has no practical purpose except to show the judge that there's no chance to rein the horse (Rule 7).

horse might block, jump and fly backward to block again, but most cutting horses just aren't up to this kind of maneuver.

Such cattle at home will sour the colt and make him lose interest. He must win most of the time to keep up his interest, so we must have cattle more suited to his style at first so that he can develop up to a really rank cow.

Rule 5. If a horse turns the wrong way with tail toward animal, he will be disqualified for that go-round with no score.

I once read an article in a horse magazine in which the author stated that if you wanted to make a cutting horse, you never let him turn his tail toward a cow, while you *would* turn tail to the cow to make a reining horse. He said that it had taken him many

Working fast and tight, Steel has gone a little out of position—too far past the cow. Lost ground must be made up or a cow might be lost.

years to learn this and that there were many good cowboys raised in the hills who had not learned this yet.

Hogwash! The only time you turn your tail to a cow is when you are tangled in your rope and stuck fast in a barbwire fence.

Turning around on a cow makes you almost automatically lose the cow and teaches the horse to work on the wrong end. The horse should plant his rear end and duck and dodge with the front end in motion. There is no question about this whatsoever.

Rule 6.   Reining and cueing penalties.

While training a cutting horse we will rein him as little as possible, as we are trying to make him a real self-worker. If we have to rein him very much at a show, we will be penalized right out of the money.

When at home, if you must rein or even pull the colt to get him into the correct head-to-head position, do it. At home it doesn't cost a cent. The horse must learn to *be there*, and you can't teach him that by letting him ramble at will anywhere he wants to go.

Since Rule 6 deals with cues, let me mention a couple of cues I use to teach the horse to fall back, when falling back is necessary to maintain working position. Many horses must be taught to back up to keep the working advantage; otherwise they will just let a cow work up farther and farther on them until the cow is so close they have lost the distance advantage, and then they lose the cow. When the colt learns to back up by himself, he will keep his leverage.

First, you obviously should have a good back-up on your colt. He must back up before he works cattle, but even so, when we back him up to maintain leverage, his head will go up too high; he'll pay so much attention to us backing him that he will forget about the cow—and she will make it back to the herd.

We solve this by teaching our colt to back to a voice cue. To start with, we lean forward and tap him on the chest with a bat while saying "back" and backing him with the reins. Soon we will be able to back him with light taps and the command "back" without using the reins. We'll work on this until we will back by voice alone. Then we work this in connection with cow work and, presto, our colt is backing to keep his working position with his head low and his eye on the cow. We use the vocal command for a while, but gradually the colt will learn what he's doing and will truly back up himself.

Some horses might get to falling off to the side (turning away from the bat). A backing collar might be the answer here. I take a piece of rope, tie a couple knots in it and loop it around the colt's neck. I fasten one end to the cinch by means of a strap and snap, so the pull will be well down on his chest and not up on his neck. A well-reined horse will handle with this rig.

Since the pull is down on his chest, he has little reason to raise his head.

Two training whips will really sharpen the back-up. A touch of the whip on the colt's shoulder will speed his back-up. Two whips, one in each hand, will keep him constantly backing straight and fast.

Rule 7.   For riding with a tight rein through a performance, a penalty will be given; for part of the time during a performance, less penalty.

Here is a quote from *General Information Regarding Cutting Horses* in the NCHA booklet:

Steel's temper is showing. A sour heifer wants to come back to the herd and is working him tight and hard. He's backed up as far as he can for he's almost in the herd. Gotta buckle down or lose this cow. Biting and striking cattle can't be frowned on too much in such a situation. If the rider quits the cow when in this position, he's made a "hot quit" and would lose points (Rule 8).

"One of the main essentials of a good cutting horse is that he works stock on a loose rein, the reins being used only when pulled up or stopped. Perfect cooperation and coordination between horse and rider is necessary."

The cutting horse must work on a very loose rein. His head must be down and free enough for him to block calves, goats and low-headed cows. When a cow sees that head with the flattened ears and scarey look, she is frightened into turning. A cutting horse can look mighty mean, but a tight rein can pull that look right off his face. If a horse doesn't have freedom of action, he can't work his best.

If we ride with a tight rein, the horse will be depending on us for his signals. When we add our own reaction-time to that of the

Another block coming up. This side view shows how a horse uses himself, getting his hocks down in the dirt, getting as much leg as possible up under himself for balance. The horse is much more able to do this with the rider's weight up off his kidneys. (Note how high his arched back forces the saddle.)

horse's, we'll be too slow to rein at the right place and the right time when the chips are down.

I would like to offer a word of advice to loose-rein riders. Let's say I am working a horse with very loose reins. When I have to pull him up, I have to pull with my hand way up high. This pulls the horse's head up and he loses sight of everything but moon, stars and high-flying birds. The cow is gone. I am disgusted with the horse for losing the cow, but the fault was all mine. Here is a solution that will at least help when working at home.

Remember that *low hands make a low head.* I can check the colt with the hand low if I use *both* hands. Let's say I am holding the loose reins in my left hand and I want to stop the horse. I can grab both reins in front of the saddle with my right hand and keep it down on the withers, letting the reins slip through it as I pull. This makes my right hand sort of a running martingale. The horse will flex his neck and bring in his nose, thereby being checked with no star-gazing. He can still see cows and get working again in a much better fashion. By practicing this way at home,

Steel works a single cow in the arena. Always staying head to head, his position with the cow is almost like a dance. Notice the similarity between the calf's position and the horse's position. The leg and body position is similar with both animals (Rule 4).

the horse won't be as likely to throw his head up when checked with one hand at a show.

The rider must use extreme care in handling his cutting horse. This loose-rein stuff is not much good when dry-working a horse. A slight contact with the mouth is best, but this means *feather light*. The horse can then get set to maneuver, which is not the case if the reins have a foot of slack one minute and are jerked up and back the next. The abrupt yank on the reins is always a surprise, and any horse will throw his head up in reaction to it.

Rule 8.   If a horse lets an animal get back in the herd he will be penalized 5 points.

Sometimes it is virtually impossible to stop a crazy kind of cow from getting back into the herd, but there are three principal reasons why a green or average horse will lose a cow:

(1) *Not falling back or working too close.* A horse must gauge cattle and be ready to fall back or jump back to maintain leverage. Here is the place to use the back-up command given without reins.

If you've been around horses long enough to savvy their facial expressions you'll appreciate this picture. Steel was concerned about losing this heifer, and had to do his mightiest work to head her. Now he's done it and she's turned away. The horse can now quit this cow and it won't be considered a "hot quit."

Let's say we have picked a cow that comes at us and wants to charge through rather than turn back. She will come either fast or cautiously, and when the horse ducks one way to head her, she'll lunge forward and try to make it back to the herd before the horse can dodge back and get in position. The horse must then make up lost ground and get head-to-head. This cow was a mistake to cut out in the first place, and the only wise thing to do is to get rid of her as soon as possible, without having a "hot" quit, which is always penalized heavily. If the cutter can make a successful block and turn her down the arena, that is the time to quit. (Often a wise turnback will allow this cow to slip through him instead of turning her back.)

(2) *Working too close to the herd.* When we cut out a cow, we should follow her well into the arena before stopping to wait for the turnback. If the horse has "his tail in the herd," there's no place left to fall back to, and the horse will be working his cut from the middle of the scattered herd. This is heavily penalized.

Steel Helmet is making a roll over his hocks to block his calf. He's handling himself very well in this picture.

Steel Helmet is ducking and dodging and has his calf set up. This is the play that scores points for the cutting horse. The calf is controlled and Steel isn't working as hard as he would if he had to make long runs and hard stops, to me the hardest part of cutting cattle.

Chances are that after a rank cow has been headed a few times she will give up and turn toward the turnback man. We can then quit her and try a cow that shows better. But should she not quit, the horse will really have to buckle down and work to keep head-to-head with the cow and stay out of the herd. When there's no place to fall back to, the horse must make up for it with very fast work and correct anticipation of the cow's next moves. He needs some luck, too.

(3) *Green horse.* If we have a good young horse started, he may make all the right moves but still not be fast and catty enough. He hasn't learned that he can speed up. He'll work right, but his turns and jump-outs will be too slow.

It takes time to make a cutting horse, and this colt should have a chance to work at home until he's speeded up. He should work cattle that he can master, and only work when he is fresh. (If we ride five miles before working cattle, the colt will not be tired, but the fine edge will be gone. After his speed and handiness come to him, he might need a little preliminary work to make him steadier and more reliable, though this depends upon the individual horse.)

When we go into the herd with horse that is a little fresh, he may make some mistakes, but he'll want to work because he wants the exercise. He can learn a lot about speeding up his turns in the few minutes he is still snorty.

If we give the colt plenty of time and patience and he still won't speed up, we'll have to resort to whip and spur. The colt should be familiar with spurs *before* working cattle. Otherwise, we may use the spur to head a cow and only succeed in getting bucked down. I say this from sad experience.

Rule 9. *When a horse heads an animal and goes past it to the degree he loses his working advantage, he will be penalized each time he does so. If a horse goes by as much as his length, he will be assessed a heavier penalty. Unnecessary roughness, such as a horse losing his working advantage to paw or bite cattle, will be penalized.*

If we work the colt too fast, we may get him overworking. When he goes by a cow, she has both a speed and distance advantage over him. I have ridden horses that went past a cow and had to turn and jump out very violently to get the cow headed; then they'd pass the cow the other way and have to repeat the whole thing. They might not lose the cow, but they give the rider an exceedingly rough ride and any judge will really tear apart such a performance.

Arena conditions may mislead a horse and make him miss his head-to-head position. A horse used to working cattle out in the hills will be fouled up when working in a disked-up arena or on sand.

The colt that goes by a little, and must violently jump back to head, must be slowed down and taught to think. We can help him at home if he is light in the bridle and responds well to body aids. This gives the rider a lot to do—rein, use cues and body weight—but such things separate the trainers from the passengers.

At home, when the colt has done a good job, get off him and fool around with him before he fidgets and tries to go to work on his cow. Let him know that he does not have to work all the time he is in the arena. When we relax in the saddle and show a lack of interest in working a cow, the horse should stand quietly. This might take a lot of mounting and dismounting, but the horse will get the idea. General cow work will also help, and tying up the horse (when all in a day's work) is beneficial. If the colt learns to work for all he is worth when he should work, and rest as well as he can when he is not working, we are doing a good job of making a real using horse.

If we buy a horse that overworks and has always done so, we have a tough proposition. The best thing to do would be to restart him on cattle, beginning with doggy ones. This will slow him down and teach him to really look at a cow and gauge her. Give him all-around cow work, driving cattle, rope work and plenty of riding. Reteaching a horse basic principles takes a lot of time and wet saddle blankets, but it's about the only way to get the horse to understand a cow.

There's a difference between overworking and setting up cattle. A horse should learn to set up his own cow, as often the turnback rider won't do this for him at a show. (If the turnback does set up all the cattle for the cutter, his horse is showing so much that the turnback gets looked at more than the cutting horse.)

King of Clubs and the author cutting cattle. King's a little cranky and is a twelve-year-old. He's cut cattle all his life and has this situation well in hand. He works cattle with his ears back as most aged studs do. He has his calf set up and is master of this situation.

The cutting horse might run along with the cow a little, but he soon gets a hair in front and turns her back. He does this every time she turns. If she's setting up good, she's ducking and dodging while the rider is scoring points. If the horse just lopes along with the cow, waiting for her to turn, he's doing *nothing* and is scoring *no points*. If the turnback continually sets up the cow, he's "boxing her in" for the cutter. This is permissible, but how it's judged depends upon conditions *and the judge*. Most judges give credit for setting up your own cow.

The important reason for setting up the cow instead of relying on the turnback to box for you is that there's no turnback when *actually* cutting in a pasture or on the range. You'd run that ol' cow for miles if your horse wouldn't set her up and drive her out. The true cutting horse should be able to do a job in the pasture as well as in the cutting arena.

Whoops, King of Clubs got behind his calf and is jumping out very hard to make up for lost ground. His head is swinging from left to right, adding to his momentum for this long jump (Rule 9).

Sometimes when a colt works too slow or doesn't work in close enough to the fence, we'll lose the old temper and work him over too much. He'll become afraid of us and really overwork, or try to run off. It is then the same old story. Lay off the colt for a few days and show him much kindness. Take off your spurs and work him on slow cattle for a while. If speed has really come down on him, we may have to resort to draw reins to hold him until he has slowed down. If he makes some right moves, show him kindness and reward him. If he's afraid of us, he'll watch his rider and not the cow.

When a colt or horse is too rough on cattle, I believe that, often, he connects working a cow with getting spurred. Let's say that the horse comes in slow to pick a cow off the fence. We spur hard to get there in time. If we spurred this hard when the colt wasn't looking at a cow, he would run, jump, buck or kick at the spur.

King of Clubs shown eating beefsteak. Not only is King an aged stud but the dumb author is working him during breeding season. King is cranky at this cutting and is taking it out on a calf. Though mares and geldings sometimes bite cattle, stallions are notorious about this bad habit. (The cure for this situation is to take a piece of baling wire and make a noseband snug enough to punish him if he attempts to bite cattle.)

Since he has the cow in front of him, he associates the spur with the cow and will leap in and strike or bite at the cow. After a lot of this, the horse may become a regular "cow-eater."

Another example: We are riding drag behind a bunch of slow cattle. When we are right behind a cow, we will hit the horse with a whip; he'll run into or go around the cow. If we hit him with spurs instead of a whip, he'll lay back his ears and bite the cow. Whenever possible we should lay off the spurs; the colt will then probably be a little less ready with his teeth. The main problem is not that the stock will be short some hide, but that the horse will get right out of working position to jump in and bite cattle. It can't be said that a horse should never bite or strike cattle, but it sure shouldn't get to be a habit.

9.

A Cutting Horse Case History

Let me give a practical example of what it's like to start a colt and finish him into a cutting horse. This student will have some bad habits that we'll have to correct. For sake of convenience, let's call him Bill.

Bill is a stallion, very rank and mischievous. We have acquired him as a three-year-old and will start his training immediately. All he knows is how to lead, in a rank sort of way (which is more like chasing the leader). He's a well-bred horse and has the necessary brains and conformation, but he's been overfed and has spent most of his life in a box stall. (That's a potent combination!) His owner sold him because he was afraid of the horse he'd raised.

We arrive to truck the horse home. He makes fools of us when we try to halter him, and we have to rope him in his stall to get any control over him. He drags us all over the place before we can get him in the loading chute and up in the truck. We're still all kindness at this point as we've had no opportunity to take the colt firmly in hand. He knows no restraint and thinks the world is his apple.

At home, we take him to our breaking pen, which is roughly circular and about sixty feet in diameter. The dirt in the pen is soft and churned up. We'll clarify a few things here and now.

To start with, we'll be mild. Remembering that this colt is very rank, we fool around with him until we can tie a soft foot-rope around his neck. The rope is about an inch in diameter and is of soft cotton. (It is a twisted cotton rope, not the braided kind used by rope spinners.) The knot we use is a bowline.

We then lay a "U" of the rope in front of the hoof we want to tie up and lead him into it. When the hoof is in the "U," we draw up the rope. We've already run the free end through the rope collar. Bill kicks at us and we pull the rope up and hold it as tight as we can keep it. (We've done this so many times before that it's easy, but it's difficult for the beginner; professional help is not amiss here.)

When Bill is quiet enough from his first flurry of fighting, we'll tie the rope with a simple, jerk-loose half hitch. The heavy soft rope doesn't come off as easily as a hard-twist rope would. Now that Bill is in sort of a dazed condition, we put a hand on the front part of the hoof and raise it up. A twist of rope around his pastern keeps the rope from sliding and burning him in the fight to follow.

Now he's standing quietly, and we're being careful and trying to hobble him. I like the soft leather, Utah-style hobbles, but the simple gunnysack hobble is the easiest to put on at this stage. The leather-style hobbles will not tighten up or fall off, though, and are the best if you can get them on. The hobbles go on around the fetlock joint and below the knee.

Now we bring in something to sack Bill out with. It's brought up gently and he's touched with it. We'll flip it around him and all over him. He'll fight as well as he can, but a little old lady could control him now, since he's hampered so much with the hobbles. He can't get away and he can't fight. He has to take it. Take it he will, and he'll get used to it. We don't lose our temper no matter how rough he gets—a colt has enough to learn here without contending with a human's temper. We pet him, talk soothingly and reward him when he stops fighting. We carry a sharp knife in case we have to cut him loose to save him.

If the colt just won't give up, throwing him is the only answer. To do this, we tie up the front leg and pull his head in the opposite direction. This, too, is a job for the experienced horseman, not for the novice.

When the horse is down, one person should hold him down while another ties his legs above the fetlock joints. If one person attempted to do all this alone, he'd be busier than a "one-armed paperhanger" and might not get the job done, at least on the first attempt.

After a horse is tied down, I like to tie his head up to a sur-cingle ring to keep it off the ground. This is an uncomfortable position for the horse, but we are trying to make it tough on him. We will not leave him in that position longer than it takes to sack him out on the ground. Once in a while, his head can be untied to let it rest on the ground, but we should keep hold of the rope so he cannot thrash around and hurt the eye. (It's a good thing to place something under his head when it's on the ground to keep dirt out of his eye.)

When he's down, we rub him just about everywhere, blow in his nostrils, get wild with the sack (though we never hit him in the face with it) and maybe shake a sackful of tin cans around him. We sit on him and pet him.

Bill isn't a real outlaw and after a while he gives up. Then we let him up, and we don't try to teach him anything else that day; the starch is out of him, and he has already been taken down a peg. He doesn't know what to make of this because he always had his own way and now he's been made as helpless as a new foal. This is all very puzzling, and we shouldn't crowd him the first day.

Next day, we'll take him to the breaking corral and hobble him again. He probably won't need the Scotch hobble first, this time, but if he does we'll put it on him. After he is hobbled, we'll sack him out a little and then slip a saddle to him. If he makes a fuss, we'll hold the saddle in place since we don't want him to get in the habit of jumping out from under this rig.

We then slowly draw up the cinch, making sure to keep hold of the saddle so he won't fight it off. We cinch it just snug enough so that it will stay on no matter what he does.

Now, if he is just hobbled in front, he may still kick, so we have a training whip with us. If he kicks, we will whip him for it and nip this habit in the bud. We'll keep the whip with us but not beat him up with it. When he kicks, one sharp cut over the rump is enough.

We have a hackamore on him, set high enough so there's no danger of shutting off his wind. We wrap the mecate a couple of turns around the horn and hold the wraps down with the rope string or strap.

We draw up the cinch some more and take off the hobbles. Most rank colts with a little age on them buck at this stage. Bill's head shoots down and he starts to fire. He gets a hard rap on the nose, though, and he gets it every time he tries to get his head down. This is pure and good horse training—he gets his punishment the very second he commits the act. It doesn't take him long to get the idea, and he's soon running around the pen with his head up. Since the pen is small and round, before long he finds that running is getting him nowhere and he simmers down and gradually stops. We walk up to him, if he'll allow us, and pet him or give him a little reward of something he likes.

If the colt just sulks when we remove the hobbles, we take it easy and wait for him to move. He'll move sometime.

Next comes the longe line. We'll hobble and saddle the colt and put a hackamore with fiador on him. A rope is tied on the mecate, and with the aid of a training whip we make him circle us. When we raise the training whip and make a short jerk with the mecate, the colt should stop. The oral command "whoa" should accompany this action. The mecate reins are again set and wrapped on the horn to prevent bucking. Should the colt buck with his head up, we can jerk him around and yell at him to make him quit. As soon as the colt will stop and start and maybe back a little, he's had enough longeing, in my opinion. There is little use in keeping this up for a long time, and we can move on to the more advanced training.

Some people like to snaffle-bit the colt during the longeing, and if this is done, the process should be a four-reined one. The head should still be held up with the hackamore and the longeing done on the snaffle bit with a light web longe line.

Now, with the longe line still on, we call in our helper. We tie the stirrups together underneath the belly and run two ropes or long lines through them to the hackamore or snaffle bit. One of us leads the colt with the longe line and the other drives him. Gradually, the driver comes to handle most of the action, with the man at the longe line standing by in case of emergency.

Bill now starts to learn to respond to the pull from the hackamore or bits. We gradually teach him how to stop, turn, go forward and back up. When we pull to turn him, we pull on one rein with short easy pulls and releases, never a steady pull. To stop him, we pull with one rein and then release, giving him the oral command "whoa." If he doesn't stop, we have the longe-line man come up and say "whoa" and give a light pull with the longe line. Remember to pull with one rein only, so that the other's in reserve to bring his nose down should he throw his head.

Since Bill is rank, he may be a little ticklish and jumpy when the rein touches his rear, especially on the turns. The longe-line man should be right on the job here to keep the whole outfit from getting tangled up. The colt will soon get used to this and pay no attention to it. When he's handling pretty well at driving, he's ready to be ridden.

Now, of course, all this doesn't happen in one day. It has taken about a week to get this far. We're careful to take plenty of time, for we don't want Bill to get the jump on us and get away with anything.

Even though we're confident of our past handling of Bill, when it comes to actually riding him we take the precaution of having our longe-line man ready. We take a fairly short hold on the left rein of the mecate, a fistful of mane along with it, and we tug on the mane a little. We ease the toe into the stirrup and hold it there. (Where we stand depends on how kicky Bill is. If he is apt to blast us, we stand where we can watch that back hoof.)

Now let's put a little weight in the stirrup and pull the weight off the ground. If all is well, we'll give him some more weight. Experience has taught us that this is an especially dangerous time of training as the colt may do anything when he feels this live weight. We go at it easily; he may start to buck or throw himself over backward. He might kick hard, wheel fast to get rid of the weight, and buck. (Without a lot of ground training he'd be certain to do something. That's why we gave him a lot of ground training.)

If Bill is still hard to get on and moves around a lot, we must keep him circling to his left with his head to us. If much of this goes on, we'll have to get along without the longe-line man, since we would just get tangled up and get in a real storm.

If we see that the colt is really going to be bad—hard to get on and hard to ride—we can bring in a snub horse and do the job from him. The snub horse should handle well and be gentle. He should also be big.

We get up behind the man riding the snub horse and crowd the colt against the gate so he can't swing out when we start to get on. A Johnson rope-halter and stout lead are good supplemental equipment to the hackamore and snaffle for this stuff. The colt is snubbed very close so he can't get enough leverage to fight. About all he can do besides what he should do is to lie down.

We ease over onto the colt and get our stirrups and reins. The colt is snubbed with about a foot of play now, and the snub horse is dragging him around. Gradually the snubber gives him more and more rope, and finally turns us loose. We ride the colt around the pen a few times, turn him and try to get him to stop. If there is no fight, we stop the ride before the horse or the rider makes some mistake. We let the snubber pick us up off the colt by riding in and snubbing up pretty close. We can get off with the bronc's head facing the snub horse's tail, or we can climb back on the snub horse by crowding the colt against a gate so he can't swing out when we climb over.

A couple of rides with the snub horse should tell us how safe it is to get on and off the colt from the ground. If he's really rank, we'll stay with the snub horse quite a while because, as with any other part of horse training, patience is the keynote.

If we've gone ahead working without a snub horse, we'll be in no hurry. It may take a little while before we can step aboard without the colt flinching. When the colt will stand, we'll get on and off a few times and then have the longe-line man come up and move him. He can lead the colt and jerk him if he tries to pitch. Soon the colt's going okay, and the helper turns us loose.

Remember, we're in the small breaking corral, so we must turn quite a bit. We'll pull the colt a little in one direction and then turn and cross over in a figure eight and go the other way. This allows us to turn the colt one way as much as the other. When we have ridden, turned and stopped, we've had a good first ride and it's time to quit. We may have a little trouble getting off. We could ride up to the helper and let him assist in stopping and holding the colt. Or we can pull the colt's head to the left and step off. As we've been off and on before moving the colt, we shouldn't have too much trouble.

As it turned out, Bill didn't buck on his first ride, and we haven't had to hurt or abuse him in any way. We make sure to ride him every day now that we have him started, because a few days off can give a colt a chance to store up a lot of meanness. We do a little more with each ride. We take care not to pull steadily on the hackamore when we work him, as this could undo all our good work.

After a few days we become accustomed to Bill and he to us. He'll try a few more things to bluff us, and we try to determine how much actual control we have over him. He may try to run with us, but we quickly correct this by doubling him. Here's how we do this:

Bill is cantering along with us when suddenly he decides to bolt and run. When he makes his first lunge, we take his head away from him with a hard pull to the side and make him sharply reverse directions. This really shakes him up, but he starts running the other way. We double him hard on the other side. We do this as often as we have to to get him stopped. When he actually stops, we pet him. We won't lose our temper and keep doubling him any more than is necessary. Hardly any colt is well enough behaved never to need doubling, but they quickly learn that their rider can double them any time he wishes. This is the secret of controlling the hackamore horse.

When loping along, we'll pull in on one rein and then release it. The colt should slow down. If he doesn't, we check him again. If there's no response to this, we double him. He should soon learn to walk, trot and lope without increasing speed until we leg him up into the desired speed. The pulling in with the single rein is called tucking. It's a good head-positioner but shouldn't be overdone.

We talk a lot while handling our colt so that he gets used to the tone of our voice. He learns "whoa," "walk," the grunt of disapproval, the hiss to back him up and the kinder tone of "attaboy" or other words of approval. The tone of voice has more influence on his response than the words do. But we never say anything like "go" to start him if we want him to stop on "whoa." They sound too much alike.

Bill's coming along all right, but one day he figures out that going into the pen means that he is going to work. He thinks that perhaps he can keep from working by balking—and balk he does. Different things work on different horses, but we first try the popper. The popper is a doubled latigo that doesn't sting much but makes a loud sound on the horse's rump. When he balks, we whack him smartly over the rump. He makes a lunge and keeps going. When he goes on in good style, we reward him for doing the right thing.

Let's say that the popper doesn't work at all. Bill has immobilized himself and is angry and sullen because we used the popper. He's dangerous now, and any attempts to move him should be made with extreme caution. The best thing to do is to get off and bring out the hobbles. We will hobble him in front and draw up a hind hoof in the Scotch hobble. Now he *can't* move, and about an hour of this should effect a cure. When he *wouldn't* move, the choice was his. By making it our choice, and taking away his freedom of choice we often solve the problem.

But let's say that when we take off the hobbles and try to move him, he still balks. Rather than lose our temper, we throw him and tie him down. We leave him down quite a while and when we let him up after this, the chances are very good that it will be a long time before we must contend with Bill balking again.

Bill has been ridden for a couple of weeks now and, along with the other new things that are constantly happening to him, it is time to get him used to the rope. We use a short, fairly limber rope for this. First we build a small loop and show it to the horse. We should make quite a production of this to assure him that we don't intend to whip him with it. Then we slowly start to swing the loop. Bill spooks at this but quiets down shortly. As soon as he is used to the loop swinging in the air, we throw it on the ground. When the loop-end is pulled toward the colt, he'll want to shy, strike at it or whirl and run away. (We may have to drop the rope to control him, so the rope is never tied to the horn at this stage.)

We'll whirl the rope some more and throw it out and drag it in. Soon the colt will allow the rope to be pulled up along his leg

A little education with the rope is never amiss for the cutting horse.

Getting Bill used to the rope and what it might catch.

and shoulder. We touch him all over with it so he won't be too spooked if the rope later touches him on the rump or gets tangled between his legs. We do a lot of this because we want any western horse we handle to be accustomed to the rope.

The next step is to drag a light log (one weighing about sixty pounds, at this stage). We find one that has some short branches for the loop to catch on, so that we don't have to get off to put the rope on it. We rope this log and let the colt get used to dragging some weight. (The rope will pat him on the rump when he is dragging the log, so we're still dallied in case he spooks and runs.) When he is used to the light log, we let him pull some heavier ones. Most horses enjoy this if it is not overdone, and no special trouble is expected.

Bill is coming along well, though he is still part bronc. He is quite responsive to the hackamore—more so than a doggy colt would be. We have to be on the alert all the time to stay with him if he jumps with us, and to double him if he spooks and runs. Now he needs riding and cow work to steady him down. The many and varied chores of a cow horse will help Bill. We're ready to put some longer rides on him, but he must be shod first.

We've handled Bill's hooves since the first saddling. The foot-rope helped to get his hind hoof up, and we can now pick up and hold a back hoof without too much fuss. He is a little worse with his font ones. If we're not going to shoe Bill ourselves, we'll still have to be there to help the horseshoer or we may never again be able to avail ourselves of his services.

First, we tie up a front leg as if we were going to throw the horse. We fool with the foot a little, and when he's standing quiet, we take off the rope or strap, and the smithy can trim the hoof. We repeat the process with the other front foot. The hind legs should be easier, but if he's still kicky, we braid a ring in his tail and hoist the hoof up. After the hooves are trimmed we let them right down. It's pretty mean to keep that hoof hoisted up there while the smithy makes the shoes.

If the shoe must be made in the forge, it's a good idea to make a cardboard pattern of the hoof and put the colt away while the shoes are being forged. A hot fit is good, but we're not interested in perfection; just getting the first shoes on the colt is enough.

If the colt is pretty sensible, it's better to shoe him without tying up his hooves. We can feed him or scratch him—even twitch him if necessary. If the colt and shoer are both patient, it can be done.

If this isn't possible, we tie up each foot as we go along; this will usually do the job. But if all else fails, we'll throw ol' Bill and nail 'em on. If he's really rank and just does not respond to training concerning his feet, throwing is the only recourse. The hooves on each side should be tied together, and a pole can be used to level the feet up into a position that isn't too tough for the shoer to work on.

So Bill has his shoes and we are prepared to put some real rides on him. Of course, we won't just start out riding him all day —rather, we'll set an hour on him at first and then build him up. If the country is flat, we can give him a lot more riding than if we go up and down hills all the time.

If we make a three-hour ride, let's cool his back at least every hour. This, of course, depends on the weather. If it's hot, we'll cool his back more often than we would in cool weather.

We check his feet after every ride. This will prevent Bill from getting foreign matter embedded in the hoof and will also make him a lot better to shoe the next time.

Checking pastures on Bill every day, we trot quite a bit to cover distance but we also try to get Bill to walk easily and softly around the cattle. He'll soon learn to "pussyfoot" through a bunch of cows without alarming them. Until he reaches this stage, we keep him outside the bunches of cows we check. He'll learn to look at a cow, slow down and get cautious when approaching cattle.

A little country cutting is never amiss at this point. Often we'll find a cow that we want to move to check her for hoof-rot or something. Bill has learned to be cautious, so we handle him and the cow easily and slowly as we move her away from her friends. We keep as much distance between cow, horse and other cattle as possible in anticipation of the cow's attempt to rejoin the bunch. Bill is held up and the cow is blocked. If the cow isn't rank, this shouldn't be difficult. A pass or two is about all she'll make and we have had a chance to see if she's limping.

Since Bill is pretty green, we should have help to take the cow

Logging the colt will teach him about weight on the rope.

Bill learns about heeling, working cattle in the hills.

in to doctor. We also need help if we rope her and treat her in the pasture. Let the more experienced horse do the fast work. If we catch her in the pasture, let the experienced horse be the head horse and we'll heel off Bill. We won't have to run him to do this. The header can then do the doctoring and we can stay on Bill and concentrate on handling him correctly and keeping that heel-rope tight. But he's had all this with a spooky log so he shouldn't be too much concerned about an old cow.

Bill doesn't know the cow enough to do much running yet, and we should be careful not to let him run. We could get in a lot of trouble if speed comes down on him. When handling rank cattle or roping where a run is required, we're better off using the old broke horse.

When we have the opportunity during the day's ride, we'll ride in a pen and lope Bill along a fence, set him up and roll him back a few times. This will keep him working on his hindquarters. We'll also lope him at a gate, once in a while, and set him up (stop him), being careful not to pull the mecate with a steady pull, just a pull and release.

Now Bill's getting pretty handy. He'll back up quite a ways and does a good figure eight. We're still pulling and not neck-reining him, but he responds to the shifting of our weight and the position of the legs. We squaw-rein once in a while, and now we see a little fault creeping in that we must correct.

The fault is ours more than Bill's. We are right handed and carry the reins predominately in the left hand. When we want Bill to roll-back, we sometimes bat him on the shoulder to speed up the turn. Since the reins are carried in the left hand, we can bat him easier on the right shoulder than on the left. To bat him on the left shoulder, we must shift the reins to the right hand and shift the bat to the left. Or, we must swing the bat in an arc over his neck, a clumsy prospect at best.

We expect the colt to be ambidextrous, to work as well on one lead as the other, but we ourselves are not ambidextrous. We must practice switching over and using the right hand for the reins.

Some may object that this is not allowed at the horse shows. Sure it isn't, but we're training a colt, not showing in western equitation. To make a colt work leads correctly, we must shift rein hands. Even if we aren't neck-reining, we use one hand more than the other for such things as using the bat and, of course, roping.

Bill has done well for us. He's pretty supple, will back straight and fast, changes leads and he stops and rolls back correctly. He also watches a cow. Since he has the necessary speed and alertness to make a cutting horse, we decide to concentrate on that.

Bill has it all over some colt that's never worked in the hills. We can skip a lot of preliminaries and get right down to cutting cattle.

We start with easy cattle and use a turnback man from the start. We want to control the work and feel that we are in little danger of spoiling the colt, since he can handle the caliber of cattle that we'll use.

We're working in a pen and have about ten head of gentle cattle held up in a corner. Bill knows better than to charge heedlessly into the herd. He learned this checking pastures. We slowly ride around and through the cattle to settle them down and get them used to the horse. The turnback man now holds the herd and pushes back the bunch-quitters. Soon they are quiet and we ease one out. We take her out into the center of the arena and stop the colt. Up to now he knows what we are doing because he has done it before.

Now we bring on the new stuff. The turnback man starts the cow back to us, and we maneuver Bill in a head-to-head position to block her. The turnback man falls back to keep from working too tight. The cow comes to us, and we head her, turn her back and hold up.

We've headed the cow and turned her back. All is well, so we dismount and let the turnback man drive the cow back into the bunch. We remount and cut out another cow, dismounting when Bill's part is done.

After four or five cows have been worked, we call it quits and breathe a sigh of relief that no cow has gotten by the colt on his first day of arena cutting.

Up to now Bill has had plenty of work in the hills and has been too tired or hasn't had the opportunity to watch another horse instead of a cow. We're now keeping him up and graining him

The finished product.

so he starts acting like a stud horse. He forgets about the cow and fusses at the turnback horse. We must punish him when he swings around and nickers at his friend. Warp him with the bat or spur him to take his mind off the other horse and put him back on the cow. This is no time to be timid, as the horse can easily get the upper hand and become rank.

Maybe Bill will not respond to this treatment and is the kind of horse that needs a lot of work. He can either go back to the hills to settle down or we can ride him enough to get him tired before we work cattle.

We're now at the stage where we have a green cutting horse that needs practice, work and patience. Too many other things come up for mention here, mainly due to the fact that each and every horse is different.

We must remember that we should reward the horse for doing a good job and punish him for doing badly. If we just silently cut out one cow after another, the colt can become bored with it all and not bother to watch the cow too closely.

The rider who can work his colt in the hills and in the pen has a strong advantage over the rider who is limited in this respect. The colt has much less chance of going stale.

CUTTING CUTTING COSTS

Friends, cutting cattle is fun. Training cutting horses is fun. Folks are missing fun that they could be enjoying because of what they have heard about the expense of maintaining a cow horse and cattle.

What makes it expensive? First, the cattle and the replacement cattle. Some people sour cattle in a couple of weeks. Then they have to replace them. This means that they must buy and sell twenty to thirty cows twice a month. This gets to be mighty expensive. Why do cattle sour so quickly?

Overwork! If you're going to let everyone in the county work your cattle, they'll sour fast. If you enjoy having a lot of people around working your cattle, you'll have to pay for it. Many enjoy this and can afford it. They buy fat two-year-olds, sour and take weight off them and replace them at a loss.

Let's see how the poor boy can do it.

First, buy young cattle and try to buy poor ones. Then they'll grow while you're using them even though they won't fatten up much. Give them good care and you might even make money on them. Worm them! No use feeding worms. Keep the flies off them. Put them in a horse stall and spray them fairly often.

If you have little pasture and have to feed, use economical local feed. Feed what is available. Check with some smart local cowman.

To keep these cattle working, work by yourself. There is always a joker in the deck, and a joker who runs cattle and plays "cowboy" will make cattle impossible to work, or "sour." You and a herd-holder who can double for a turnback man are enough.

So if your cattle feel good and you don't sour them with overwork, they should last quite some time, especially if you have but one cutting horse.

If your only horse is your cutting horse, you can get turnback help when you need it from someone on foot. A man just standing down arena, waving an arm once in a while, can be a big help when your cows get too gentle to furnish much play.

The size of the arena is important. The larger the pen, the fresher the cows will stay. Nothing sours cattle like working in a small inside arena. You can gentle cattle inside in one session.

A big pen and/or pasture cutting will teach a colt to set up his own cattle. This is pretty vital. A small pen will teach a colt to work off his hocks. The cow can't run as much in the small pen and will be more apt to duck and dodge. A horse really needs both kinds of work, so it's not a bad idea to build two pens. The small pen could be forty to fifty feet wide and a hundred feet long. The larger pen should be about sixty-five feet wide and two hundred feet long.

This doesn't sound very wide, but when your colt must run back and forth to head running cattle, it'll seem much wider. I don't see much reason in a pen wider than sixty-five feet. I'd rather cut in a pasture than a really wide pen.

Pens to work in, though an initial expense, will last for a long time, so build good high ones. Often cattle will be a little panicky when worked for the first time, and they are less apt to come out of a six-foot fence than a five-foot fence. After being worked a couple of times, practically all cattle will lose their initial fear.

So the pens are built and the cattle are purchased. If you buy the cattle right, chances are they won't cost you much.

Now for the horse. I hope you buy a good gelding. A gelding, not having sex to worry about, makes a good, reliable, ever-ready cow horse. Buying a colt with "cow in his pedigree" will help. Of course, training your own horse will help financially. If you need to take the colt to a trainer for a few months on cattle, perhaps you could have him going well enough for the trainer to go right on with him.

Just a word about cutting clubs. There are people who buy cattle together and have regular cutting sessions. This is a "share-the-expense" deal that works very good under certain circumstances. The main thing is that you shouldn't join such a group and expect to train your cutting horse at the sessions. You should train him at home and take him to such a cutting to cut under actual contest conditions. If everyone who joins such a group goes there to train their horses, bedlam will result. Cattle will be immediately soured, horses will be spoiled and ill feeling will be the end result.

For instance, one rider will want to do the right thing. He'll go into the herd, cut a few cattle, use no more than regular contest time and ride out satisfied. Another guy will go in, chase cattle for fifteen minutes and ruin things for everyone else. Make sure, before joining such a group, that you are not joining up with a bunch of "heel flies."

Abide by definite rules. Run a get-together like a regular cutting. It needn't be judged, but limit the time in the herd to two and one-half minutes. The "wild ones" won't like this, and they'll stop coming. The people who appreciate a nice session will then come regularly. These clubs should just simulate a regular contest and no more. If run right, these get-togethers are a fine thing, and I wish every town had such a place available.

Owning a pleasure cutting horse is a hobby. All hobbies cost a little money. By keeping costs down, cutting will cost no more in the long run than golf or photography.

10.

Smoothing Out Spoiled Horses

THE MIXED-UP COLT

I sometimes get a colt that the novice horseowner has tried to break himself (no training fee for him). Now just watch the local talent go to work:

This fellow generally has no idea of what he wants the colt to do. He has no starting gear and wouldn't know how to use it if he had it. With Aunt Minnie and all the relatives helping, he manages to get his rig cinched down. On goes the long-shanked curb bit. With Aunt Minnie holding on for all she's worth, this guy climbs on and the ball opens up.

He is scared so he holds the reins tight and hurts the colt.

It's all over soon. Mr. Horseowner is laying all stretched out. His wife is fanning him and Aunt Min's getting the smelling salts. They've phoned for the ambulance.

The colt is over in a corner, all wide-eyed. He doesn't savvy this. He has got a sore or broken mouth. Maybe the bars are injured. It doesn't take much to break them down, and Mr. Bronc Rider was sure pulling.

The hospital releases ol' Bronc Rider in a few weeks taped up like a mummy. He groans and moans around quite a while and collects unemployment insurance. The wife and Aunt Min take turns waiting on him because he sure had them afraid that they'd lose the breadwinner.

So this guy, who goes to church on Sunday, hunts up a horse trainer. What he tells the trainer doesn't go too well with what he's learned in church, for he says that he has a nice, green colt that hasn't been fooled with. He'd never think of breaking his own colt as he believes a plumber should plumb, a dentist should pull teeth and a horse trainer should train horses. No, the colt is nice and gentle and no one's been on his back. All this because the guy that recommended the trainer told him that the trainer likes his colts unridden and charges extra for spoiled ones.

Now let's say that I'm the trainer this guy takes his colt to. I'm suspicious because he has emphasized the fact that the colt is unridden. (It's the truth; nobody's made a ride on him yet.) So what I do is go right back to letter "A" and review the whole basic training procedure.

I work the colt out on the ground. I break him to hobbles and sack him out. This all goes well and when I feel that he's had enough, I get on. That head's up, one ear's laid back and he's looking back at me sitting there in the saddle. He's humped up and ready to blow the plug. I see he's been hurt in the mouth and is set to fight back.

Now if I want to fight a horse and do some bronc riding, I have one that's ready. Only thing is, that's a poor way to get him going. He needs to have a little confidence in the rider, so I give the colt Round One and climb off. He didn't get away with anything as all I did was get on, sit there and get off.

The next step is to get the colt moving, turning and stopping as quietly and gently as possible, so I resort to the longe line. From experience, here's the rig I use.

I pad a limber hackamore by wrapping the noseband and sides with soft cloth so I won't skin him up. I use a fiador so the hackamore won't slip off his chin. I affix my hair rope or other suitable rope to this. The rope should be at least twenty feet long—thirty feet is better.

Putting this rig on the colt, I make him travel in circles around me, first one way, then the other. I teach him about "giddap" and "whoa." I take plenty of time and am patient at this stage. If I louse it up here, it'll be very tough to get this colt going. If he learns slowly, okay, because he's had a bad start and is confused and frightened.

After I'm satisfied with his progress, I drive him in long reins to get him used to turning. He'll start when I cluck to him and stop when I say "whoa," so chances are it won't be too tough.

I use my saddle when I drive the colt, as I sometimes like to get right on and ride after the driving if everything goes all right. I hobble my stirrups so they won't pull up or flap, then run a rope or strap from snaffle or bosal through each stirrup. Now I'm ready to drive the colt. It's nice, though not essential, to have a helper at this stage of the game in case the colt becomes frightened and blows up. He can stop the colt from the front in case we get in a storm. He holds a rope attached to the head gear so he controls the horse from the longe line position.

I'll teach the colt quite a bit about plow-reining and stopping, and if all goes well, I'll ease on and ride. The colt knows the commands, so the rest shouldn't be too tough. How far I go from here depends upon the horse and his owner. Getting the colt going is practically assured. If I do have trouble, I look for physical reasons, such as sore back or unsoundness. There is always the chance that the colt might be loco. A sign of this is the constantly weaving head—"snake hunting."

When the colt is going all right and he's ready to turn back to his owner, a little instruction never goes amiss, unless he's the type of guy you can't tell anything—and there are plenty of these. I have him ride the colt and watch and offer advice. This can often be done diplomatically and with no hard feelings on either side. The trainer must often be a diplomat as he deals with two-sided ignorance, the colt's and the owner's.

DOWNHILL

Many people like to raise their own colts and have them trained. They figure they'll then have a horse bred and trained the way they want him to be. Most folks who have done this get the colt home again and watch it slide *downhill* from a well-trained colt to a horse with many bad habits. The trainer is often blamed for this by the unknowing. More often it's the horse-owner's own fault and is caused by his own bad riding habits.

I believe that the biggest single fault in the horse is highheadedness, and the high hands of the average rider are the biggest single reason for it. This is much more prevalent among western horsemen than among their English riding brethren. The western rider has the high fork and horn of his saddle to contend with. At best, his rein hand is held at horn height that puts the hand at least seven inches above the withers. If the reins come out the top of the hand, add at least four inches to the seven, and we have the reins held a foot above the withers. The old axiom "low hands make a low head" is very true.

A good hackamore man can get a low head-set on a horse when he is using a hand on each rein. He can get his hands low and keep them there. If he neck-reins in the hackamore, the horse's head starts up, his stop becomes poor and he works out of position.

Many people force their horses to work on the wrong end. They actually train the horse, by incorrect work, to stop and turn on the front legs.

A common drill that many riders employ is to lope down the fence and roll the horse back over his hocks. The colt just back from a good trainer will do this in fine shape. As the owner continues to work his horse on this exercise, he finds that the horse gets worse and worse and is turning on his front legs. The owner drills more and more to correct this and the colt gets worse. Finally, he must take a spoiled horse back to the trainer for correction.

What the owner did wrong was a sin of omission. He neglected to put the "whoa" in the roll-back.

The "whoa" is called the "dwell." The dwelling horse is the horse that does a good slide and roll-back. He must definitely pause between slide and turn or he must turn on his front legs. The pause can be minutes or a fraction of a second. The front hooves must hit the ground before the turn signal is given. The front legs furnish the impulse for the turn.

Once the horse has learned to turn on his front legs, correction is difficult. He must learn to turn the right way without a spur in the shoulder because he may only associate turning on his back legs (rolling over his hocks) with a spur in the shoulder. Judges of reining classes take a dim view of this.

Instead, take the horse along the fence and stop four or five

A soft-mouth rubber Pelham with running martingale. I often use this rig to help the horse keep a better head position. It's a very good rig to use when roping since the rider's hand is often too high then—it's unavoidable. The running martingale really shouldn't be used on the curb rein, but, roping, it's better than the very high hand we use.

feet away from and parallel to the fence. You should use a hackamore or some form of colt bit for this, because you will pull the rein, not neck-rein him.

Pull the colt quickly into the fence and jump him out. You forced him to turn on his hind legs—if you turned him fast enough. Let him run in small circles until he's calmed down. If you drilled him for a right turn, drill him the same way for a left turn.

Of course, the colt won't immediately start working off his hocks. This drill needs deliberate, daily repetition, but never drill, drill, drill! The horse becomes angry at too much of this and you'll lose what you've gained. Roll him back and circle for

Ken Sirco is trying here to show a horse working out of position. The mare is loping to the right. She's on the right lead, but is bent to the left. Ken has a hard neck rein on her. The pull of the indirect rein forces her into this awkward position.

a while. Let him walk around and blow. Work the other side, circle and blow. If you overwork the colt and teach him to hate the roll-back, he'll learn to side-pass so close to the fence that you can't work him. If you work too close to the fence, you'll teach him to rear.

If he rears, you should double him (using a hackamore or colt bit) immediately. Remember, doubling is pulling hard on one rein to spin him forcefully around in his tracks. If he "sticks" and "bulls" so that you can't double him, get off quickly and run a rope from hackamore or colt bit to the cinch or to a big ring tied to a back saddle-string or back cinch-ring. A hard pull and release on this rope will double the colt and limber his neck so that he can be pulled from the saddle in the future. If the colt keeps "sticking" (fillies also often do this when in heat) it's wise to keep a big ring tied onto your saddle just for this purpose.

Here Ken shows us the way many folks try to stop their horses. We see people ride like this in every horse show we go to. What's wrong? (1) Ken's hands are way too high. (2) He is trying to stop with both hacka-more reins pulled at the same time. (3) He's leaning back, which caves in the mare's back. (4) The reins are coming from the top of his hand, not the bottom, which makes the pull even higher. (Ken felt so bad about treating the mare this way for the photo that he gave her an extra ration of feed and much sweet talk.)

Many old-timers tie the colt's head around to his tail to limber him up, but this will not serve the purpose as well as the pull and release. The colt will fight when his head is tied to his tail. This cramps his neck, especially if he's left long in this position. He might fall and, at the least, skin his nose and chin with the hacka-more. Nor will he learn to give his head as well as he would if his head were just pulled hard and then released.

When the colt has learned to "set and turn," a full circle can be worked like this:

Stop the colt five feet from and parallel to the fence. Turn him into the fence. By now he should know how to turn 180 degrees fast. Do not let him jump out. Catch him when his hooves hit the ground and whirl him 180 degrees away from the fence to com-

Note the difference between Ken's stop and this stop of Steel Helmet. I'm using one hand but am "squaw reining" the horse—working the left rein with the right rein loose. I'm up off the seat of the saddle, which allows Steel to get his hind legs up under him. Since we're going fairly fast I'm spurring him a little as a collection signal. (Leg grip alone would be enough signal at a very slow speed.)

plete a circle. Jump him out as you did when working the half-circle. He has placed his hooves correctly. This should be practiced daily until he'll do a snappy circle and jump out. This is the start of the spin with the horse placing his hooves correctly. If the horse has a cloppy spin already spurred or whipped onto him, you can in time develop this haphazard stuff into a good spin.

You must remember, however, when you get impatient with his progress, that it took a long time for him to learn the wrong way. You can't correct bad work overnight.

Many people sour the reining horse by working him too much on the reining pattern. They'll figure-eight a horse so much that he'll sour on it and never change leads right. They've heard that "practice makes perfect." This isn't always the case with the reining horse. Once the horse has learned *how to*, he'll stay sharp much longer working out in the hills or pastures.

I believe that the person with a small plot of ground and no pastures to ride in has two strikes against him when he starts. He should become acquainted with someone who does have some acreage. He could help work cattle and check fence to be appreciated and not make a nuisance of himself. Horses need some room and a change quite often, and the horse-owner should furnish this, even if he must trailer his horse.

A reining horse that works in a pen all the time learns to "Scotch" or cheat his rider. He'll not want to stop, so the rider must strong-arm him more and more all the time. He'll cheat on his figure eights by changing leads before he should, after he should, or change in front and not behind.

But you can take the same horse in the pasture and lope him around an oak tree on the left lead, change leads and circle a log on the right lead. If the pasture isn't too level, he'll have to watch his footing. If nothing else, this will make him much more likely to change leads when he should. Also he'll forget about "Scotching" if he's doing something interesting.

A horse can be retaught. Many trainers teach a horse to rein without teaching much in the way of leg aids. I use leg aids on every horse and teach the owner how to use them. I can make my horses take either lead without turning them any special way when loping out. This is the simplest thing in the world if it is done consistently. It soon becomes as natural as using the clutch and gear shift when driving a car. You can correct many faults by teaching the horse leg aids.

Spurs emphasize leg aids. My spurs are very dull. I simply push the spur lightly against the horse where the leg normally hangs. Most horses do not mind this and will not switch their tails in agitation. Spurs used in this fashion are good. Tearing up a horse with spurs is not good and makes a tail-wringer. Once in a blue moon a colt will come along that will not pay any attention to a spur lightly applied. More force must be used here. Good judgment should also be used.

The reining horse that goes downhill with his backing is losing his suppleness. He'll soon go downhill in other ways too. First signs are crooked backing and head-tossing.

The horse needs to be collected to back straight and fast. I signal him by squeezing him with both legs, getting my weight in the stirrups and pulling with light tugs on the reins. I time the squeezes and pulls with his steps. After the horse has become accustomed to this, you can speed up the signals and the horse will "fly back." Correcting bad backing can best be done by practicing this method of backing. In most cases, when the rider's haphazard methods are corrected, the horse will back just fine.

If the horse has been spoiled to the extent that good riding practices won't help him back, results are best accomplished by backing him from the ground.

Rig to drive. Tie the stirrups (hobble) beneath the horse. Run two ropes from colt bit or hackamore (never curb bit) through the stirrups and drive the colt. Sometimes it's best if a rein is affixed to the saddle so the horse can't get his head way down. Drive the colt around for a while, then stop and back. Be patient but forceful if you need to be. He'll back in this rig because the reins are very low and you have lots of leverage since you are pretty well anchored. A few sessions of this and he'll back in good form from the saddle.

The methods outlined here are designed to get away from brute force. Yanking, sawing, cussing and spurring accomplish nothing but bad feeling between horse and rider. A little work the right way will tune up the ol' pony and get you back in competition again.

11.

Taming the Rank Ones

THE BUCKING HORSE

I was once breaking horses with a man whom I considered
to be very good. One day I noticed a colt buck with him, and
to my surprise he let out a yell and *cowboyed* that bucking colt.
He never tried to pull him up but rode that colt with his hackamore reins loose.

That evening we talked to the colt's owner, an old cowman. He
was perturbed when he heard that his colt bucked and asked my
friend why he had allowed the colt to pitch. My friend, who was
a talker as well as a doer, told him that the colt caught him off-
guard but he had turned him into the fence and made him stop.
He assured the cowman that the colt wouldn't be allowed to buck
in the future.

Sure enough, the colt didn't buck again, but it wasn't because
his rider didn't give him the opportunity. He had a free head and
open spaces. The colt just stopped bucking.

Since then, I have heard of many horsemen who say they never
allow their horses to buck. I have seen strange rigs to hold a
horse's head up, and I have heard riders tell of spinning the horse
to keep him from bucking.

I once had many green range colts to break. This was a mo-
notonous job, as the colts weren't rank and didn't need to be finished to perfection. They were range colts, though, and once in a
while one of them would pitch a little. I was a little bronco, too,
and had a slight interest in riding the rough ones, so I didn't object at all. I had no one around to tell me not to allow those colts

to buck, so when one did hop a little, it was a welcome relief from boredom.

I never went after one of those colts too hard when he bucked. I didn't want to scare the buck out. I was too much horseman to encourage it.

The trouble was that after a few rides, none of those colts wanted to buck anymore. It seems like they didn't have a thing to become fighty about. I didn't yank or beat them and I also didn't ride around holding up their heads. They all gentled out very nicely.

We had a stud on that outfit that was quite a fighter. He was mean to handle on the ground and could buck pretty fair and would do so at unexpected times and places. No one was anxious to use him as you never could tell when he would make you "meet your shadow."

This stud struck me once and got a whipping for it. I didn't really go after him, but just spanked him carelessly with my rope. When he kind of got the idea that I wasn't afraid of him, his attitude toward me changed and he was a good one as far as I was concerned. As long as I handled him recklessly, he gave me no trouble. I liked him because he was a fearless horse, very sure-footed, fast and tough.

Others fared no better with him than they had before I started riding him. They would be choking the horn to stay with him while I could throw my rig on him and go work cattle or rope. They were too careful, and he knew they were afraid of him.

I have never seen a colt or spoiled horse come out of the bucking habit successfully with the "not allowing" deal. If he had the buck in him, no matter how careful the rider, sooner or later he would catch the rider unaware and buck, often with disastrous results.

If you have to keep a tight rein on a horse all the time, he will never be worth a nickel. He gets hard in the mouth or on the nose. He is insensitive and becomes a hardheaded nothing. Relax the reins and he runs or bucks.

Suppose we acquire a bucking horse. If he is bad enough, rodeo producers will want him. If he isn't that bad, we can ride him or find someone who can.

If he's worth the effort, let's break him the only way I know of. That is, just to whip the buck out of him.

He ought to be in good shape when he's worked on. You never accomplish anything with a poor horse. A not-so-good rider might be able to handle a poor horse, but it will take a top one to do so when the horse is in good shape. So let's get that horse fat and we'll save ourselves a lot of grief.

The cure is simply to offer punishment when the horse is doing his worst. Whippings before or after bucking accomplish nothing. He must be pitching high, wide and handsome with the rider on him whipping for a cure to be accomplished. If we can whip him on the nose, one or two applications should do it, but we should be prepared to inflict more punishment should the need arise in the future. He should be whipped every time he bucks, not just once or twice. Notice, I said *whip*, not beat up!

If the rider is clever enough to whip the bucker on the nose, he will get the job done and the horse will get his nose up and keep it there. Our bucker will be transformed into a good, useful animal.

When we get him cured, let's show him that it's not so bad being a saddle horse. We won't give him too tough a ride and we won't yank and saw at his head. We'll lift the rig and cool his back when he is hot. We'll feed him right and take care of his feet.

Good care and attention will often work wonders to gentle a so-called "mean" horse. Chances are, the horse has had bad owners and has learned to distrust and fear man. Kindness and "ol' man time" will help us gentle and care for this type of horse, but, of course, the first thing is to be able to sit on him.

If all else fails, it would be wise to resort to throwing and tying the horse down. This is the universal cure for all really bad habits. There is a big difference between playful "crow-hopping" and real bucking. The "hopping" horse can easily be cured. The hard bucker requires drastic measures, for he will put anyone down when they're not expecting it.

The really mean horse that is a confirmed bucker has one place —it's in rodeo. Rodeo producers are always looking for a top bucking horse that can "really turn on." The producers aren't hard to find; they're all over the country. Don't let a really bad horse hurt you. Sell him to a guy who wants him—the rodeo producer.

THE KICKER

Not long ago I read an article by a well-known horse trainer who advised that a kicking horse could be cured by tying a rope from the hackamore, through the stirrup, to the offensive hoof. When the horse kicks, he punishes his nose. The author failed to mention what the results can sometimes be when such a rig is used, for if a horse kicks with much force, he may severely injure his nose. This damage could cause a permanent, unsightly lump and ruination of a light-nosed hackamore horse. If he really turns loose, he could break his nose. I once saw a colt throw a "whingy" in such a rig. The nose cracked and infection set in. After much treatment, this fine-headed horse ended up with a heavy, thick, unsightly "camel" nose.

Such treatment might be warranted for a cheap, vicious horse —but there are other, safer ways. In other words, this is not *the* treatment for kicking horses.

A better cure is to use the ordinary breeding hobble. Make sure the gear is stout and in good repair. Affix it in a snug position. Go back of the horse and make him want to kick. He can't. He'll jerk his neck and other leg when he tries.

The best rig for a kicking horse, however, is the Scotch hobble.

There are many ways to Scotch a horse. Some people advocate affixing a rope to a strap buckled around the pastern. Swell, I say, but if the horse kicks, how are you going to buckle on the strap? Here's my method.

Take fifteen or twenty feet of *soft-twist* cotton rope, about an inch in diameter. Tie a loop around the horse's neck (bowline knot) with one end. Drop the rope in a U in front of the leg you want to tie up. Lead the horse up until he steps into the U. Draw up the leg and tie the rope through the loop tied around the horse's neck. The rope should come up over and down through the loop instead of up and under. This is much easier to hold if the horse kicks.

Now we have the hoof drawn up, *not quite* as high as we finally want it. We then take hold of the hoof, pull it up a little and bend the rope once around the pastern. This prevents a burn as well as making more certain that the horse doesn't kick loose, since he can still kick forward a little.

Some people advocate a cross Scotch hobble; that is, tying up the foot on the opposite side from that you want to work on. If you are saddling a wild colt, you would Scotch up the right hind hoof. The reason: he can still kick forward a little with his scotched hoof but would fall should he kick with the other hind hoof.

Cross-hobbling is good for saddling but is of little use for shoeing, grooming or doctoring. It is a little more difficult, so for most practical purposes, I don't cross-hobble.

It's a bit awkward to shoe a horse that is Scotch-hobbled. It's hard for the smith to get in the right position. He can still get swatted lightly, but the horse can't really wind up to kick.

A better deal for shoeing is to braid a ring in the horse's tail and draw the hind hoof to the ring. This was a common practice when the western riding fever hit the country and many horses shipped east were hard to shoe. The good shoers didn't fool with a kicker. They tied his hoof to his tail. If he was really rank, he was thrown.

When Scotching or tying the hoof to the tail, use a knot that can be easily and quickly undone, as a person can get in some mighty messes. The horseman should *always* carry a sharp knife. It can save injuries to both horse and handler.

For example, we get a horse to break and want to handle his hooves and pull his tail After we get him scotched up, he turns crazy and never stops kicking. He's kicked across the Scotch rope and is in danger of getting badly rope-burned. He's kicking and flopping all over the place. He's kicking the rope so hard the knot has slipped and is too tight to untie. Out comes the sharp knife to cut the rope. Mr. Wild Horse is freed before he's badly burned and we can resort to our throwing rig to subdue the horse—all made possible because we always carry a sharp knife.

THROWING THE HORSE

The old-time horse handlers put up with most kickers and buckers and didn't take the time to Scotch-hobble them. If the horse was bad, fine; they were bad too. If the horse got too rough, though, they'd use the old tried-and-true method of subduing a vicious horse—they'd throw him and tie him down.

The horse has two resources for self-preservation. The first is flight; the second is fight. Horses do both well. A horse in good health can run away from any other animal on the continent. True, a cougar or bear may sneak up on a horse and jump him, but they can't run very far and make a catch. The horse has learned to fight such animals. Few creatures have the effective weapon of the punch of those hooves.

The rank horse can be made to surrender to man if his two methods of self-preservation are taken from him. If he can't run or fight, he gives up. I won't say that this is effective one hundred per cent of the time—horses amaze me every day. I will say that in my years of training horses I have never seen it fail when done *properly*.

How can a horse be prevented from running or fighting? Simple. Throw him and tie him down. Show him how helpless he can be made to be. If done correctly, this will work on kickers, buckers, biters, strikers, rearers—you name it. After using it on a rank horse I am always regretful that I waited so long before applying it.

How can one throw a horse? First, though, let's discuss safety to the horse. We need a breaking pen and a footing of sand, or at least soft ground. No rocks, please. A solid fence is best for complete safety. A blanket to lay under the horse's head is a good precaution to keep sand or dirt out of the horse's eyes.

I've thrown many a horse accidentally. Hobble the horse with a hobble such as the Utah on the front legs. Then Scotch-hobble a back leg up. If there's much of a fight, the horse will go down. One man and a helper can then safely tie down the horse by tying the free hind leg to the Utah hobbles.

If he acts rank in these hobbles but won't go down, tie a soft

Throwing the horse with the Scotch hobble. This is the method I like the best, and it seems to be the safest for the horse and handler. In Step 1, the near hind foot is tied up, fairly high. Next step—not shown because I was too busy actually putting the horse down—is to Scotch-hobble the other hind leg. Horse sets down, the rope is tied off and horse is pushed over, ready to be tied down.

The horse has just been thrown. The nice part about this method is that the horse is now unable to kick as he often does when other methods are used. The handler can now tie off his legs at leisure.

First Utah Hobble applied.

Both Utah hobbles applied. If the horse is very rank, hobbles should be tied together with a short rope. Hobbles should now be tightened as much as possible.

A blanket is placed and kept under the head as a cushion and to keep sand, dirt and other objects out of the eye.

Here Jimmy is flapping a slicker to "sack out" the horse. If she thrashes a lot, a helper should be on the halter rope to ease the head down. The horse will fight periodically and should be left down until these spasms cease.

rope (easier on the hands) to the Utah hobbles and jerk his front legs away when he lunges. This will also teach him not to run when hobbled.

Another method is to Scotch-hobble a back leg. Then quickly Scotch-hobble the other hind leg. He will sit down like a dog and can easily be pushed over. It's easy to tie him down when you already have the hind legs tied up.

The blanket is then place under the horse's head. I use a feed sack or slicker to sack the horse out. He will moan as he struggles to free himself. I sit on him lightly, slap all over his body, blow in his nose, rattle some rocks in a tin bucket—most anything to get him used to anything. Some men whip a horse when he's tied down. This is cruel and not necessary at all. He's going through enough without that.

I think it's wise to leave the horse tied down at least an hour.

The photographs used for illustration were taken by myself while in the process of throwing a filly. I had a valuable camera around my neck during the whole proceeding. My assistant, Jimmy Lee Thomas, only had the leadrope and waved the slicker.

This filly's problem was resentment. As long as things went her way, she was fine. When forced to work, she would try to run away and/or rear. After one treatment I feel that she would do well in a western pleasure class. She might eventually need a few more treatments, but for the present she has submitted completely.

I threw this filly and tied her down for two hours. While down we subjected her to a flapping slicker, sat on her and even discharged a revolver close to her. We hobbled the legs on each side to avoid the trauma ropes would cause. I don't feel that hobbles are necessary when tying a horse down for a short period of time. However, a rope, no matter how soft, will cut off circulation if the horse is tied down for a half-hour or more.

If there appears to be much swelling of the legs the next day, cold water applications are correct. Exercise will also help reduce the swelling. A bland diet, such as half bran and half oats, will be appropriate.

This is an old-time cure that works, but don't use it unless you really need it. Use it if you have a rank horse and you'll change him for the better. Use it with caution so that neither you nor the horse will suffer for it.

THE BALKER OR SULKER

Nothing is more provoking or dangerous than the balker. When the saddle horse balks, all the cajoling, offers of feed or whippings will fail to move him. His head goes down, ears flatten, legs are widespread, tail is tucked and a vicious expression appears on his face. If you think you can move him, you're only fooling yourself.

If you try to whip it out of him, he may suddenly throw himself on you. He's mad clear through, and it doesn't pay to fool with him.

Now this horse is seemingly immobile, but he knows he can move if he wants to. He just refuses to do any more work and will stay there or fight; he doesn't care which.

To cure him, let's really immobilize him. We'll have to throw him, and as he is mad clear through, he'll fight going down. We want to make certain our equipment is in good repair.

Maybe he really fights, but we get him down and tied up. At this point, some trainers whip the horse. Others leave him there all day. Both methods are, in my opinion, unnecessary, as they are too rough. He needs punishment, but not that severe.

Let's just make it uncomfortable for him while he's down. We'll tie up his head off the ground near the right surcingle ring. Having his head in this position for ten minutes will be very uncomfortable and long enough.

Having his head up off the ground prevents him from thrashing around and perhaps knocking out an eye on a pebble, so it's a humane thing as well as a punishment.

One application of this will work and the horse will move off for you, but the act eventually may have to be repeated. Don't hesitate. If the horse balks, throw him and you'll save yourself much concern and possible injuries.

Sometimes the balker will lie down and refuse to get up. Still, the horse knows he can get up to run or fight. He isn't so immobilized that he wouldn't rear up and run if something frightened him.

So let's tie him up as we do a regular balker. We may tie up the head if we wish, but by making it impossible for the horse to get up, we effect a cure.

Perhaps we have a horse that isn't a true balker. We may have a barn-sour horse or a horse-sour horse. This animal may refuse to leave the barn or another horse. I have effected cures by a variety of methods, often trying in desperation any cure that came to mind.

Once I was riding a good horse that had been badly spoiled. He'd been allowed to return to the barn when he refused to go forward. He'd been whipped, and this hadn't helped.

This horse would back readily, so when he refused to move forward, I backed him until he'd go forward. But after a week or so of this, the horse would back a mile and then still refuse to go forward. He wasn't mean about it; he just wouldn't go forward.

One day he really refused to move, and I got down my rope and threw loops at the ground to accustom him to the rope (taking advantage of every opportunity). I dragged the loop all over him and he didn't object. Then I laid the loop over his rump and behind him just above the hocks and pulled. This horse had been taught to lead by such a procedure and moved right off. So, when the horse balked, I would get my rope down and drape the loop around his rear. A quick pull and he'd move right off.

After a couple of weeks of this and a thousand laughs from other riders who witnessed this proceeding, he balked at the rump rope too. This made me disgusted and I rapped him with the loop. He moved right off. The length of the loop caught him down along the hind leg, lower than a bat or quirt ever reached, and this did the trick. I carried a long training whip and only had to use it a couple times. When he quit balking, he started to watch a cow and learned to take a good rein. He made a fine horse.

I don't mean that everyone should drape a loop around his balker's rump to move him. I don't mean that a person should always carry a long training whip. I am, however, trying to put across the point that there is no set pattern for horse training. Anything that works is the right method, and the trainer must try odd things when conventional methods fail him.

12.

Accidents and Their Prevention

I guess I'm entitled to write something on this subject for I've been riding other folks' horses for more than twenty years and have never been seriously hurt. I try to take very few chances. I try to bypass danger. The chances that many novice horseowners take make me shiver. My odds would soon run out if I were to be so careless.

To begin with, I have good gear and keep it in repair. I check my latigos for wear and condition. My cinches are fairly new and are regularly washed. My bridles, hackamores, reins and hobbles are kept clean, saddle-soaped and repaired. Rotten gear is replaced.

I have good facilities for handling colts and spoiled horses. Many times spoiled colts come to me because their owners tried to break them with poor or no facilities. They saddled, bridled and got on as if the beginning colt was an old gentle saddle horse.

I have a good breaking pen sixty-five by seventy feet with a six-foot fence. The colt receives gradual training that culminates in his first ride. When he goes well in the breaking pen, he graduates to the arena, which is sixty-five by two hundred feet. It may be a month before the colt is ridden out in the pastures. This depends on whether I feel that the colt is ready for it, not because some friend wants me to go for a ride with him.

Most novice horseowners feel safer when using a curb bit rather than regular colt equipment. This is a mistake. If the colt takes fright, bucks and/or runs, they must attempt to handle him with a leverage bit. The unaccustomed pain causes the colt to react violently. The end result may be the colt running, falling or throwing himself with his rider. You can manhandle a colt with a hackamore or colt bit and cause him no real pain or injury. The person who trains his own colt should learn what colt training equipment consists of and how to use it. This can be learned from books if practical observation and practice is impossible.

Training horses leaves no room for "horseplay" on the part of the trainer. It's a deadly serious business; I'd rather get soaking wet from a sudden thundershower than run my colt back to the barn. This isn't the way most folks think, and they do a good job spoiling their colt. This is easy to do and is often done by those who should know better. Running back to the barn is "standard operating procedure."

Running a horse must be a lot of fun. I hear such statements as, "If I can't run my colt when I want to, I'd just as soon sell him." The trainer doesn't think like this. I run a horse in the arena to teach him something, not just "for the fun of it." He runs in circles to learn how to handle himself, take his leads, steady himself and for muscular development. He runs to head a cow or follow a calf. This is all controlled running and is desirable. An uncontrolled run down the road is undesirable and will result in speed coming down on the colt.

The owner often pushes his colt into something with little or no training such as roping a calf or working a cow the first time the colt has ever seen a calf or cow. Not only can this foul up the colt's training for a long time, but it can also be downright dangerous. The horse working the cow can fall over the cow because he has no idea of how to work or how to avoid a tangle. The man roping off an untried colt runs so many risks that there's no use discussing them.

Let's consider and discuss some other unnecessary risks:

The loose or worn-out cinch allows the saddle to slip. Any horse will react violently if a saddle turns under him. The danger to the rider is a serious fall. The danger to the horse is that the saddle under him will craze him. He's apt to run through a barbwire fence or over a cliff. Make sure your saddle fits and is snug, then check it once in a while during a ride. Even if it's tight at the start of a ride, the saddle will settle on the horse and the horse will gaunt up, causing the loose cinch.

Many things can cause a runaway. You're on a potential runaway every time you take a colt out of the arena. Make sure that you can handle him well enough to get him stopped, or at least get him running in tight circles under any circumstances. Never hackamore a colt in the open if you can't bend his neck. The safest rig I know of to stop a colt is draw reins on a colt bit.

Many people, if they are to ride at all, must ride on a public road. I have no suggestions for them except that they should learn to pray and should ride only gentle old plugs. When I am driving a car and approach a rider on the road, I slow up to creep around the horse, being ready to stop instantly if the horse should shy in front of me. Most people never slow up or ease to give the rider room. Some maniacs even blow their horns, yell at the horse and beat on the side of the car, intentionally frightening the horse. There ought to be a law.

Having a horse fall on you is a serious thing. This has often happened to me. A horse will slip while working a cow. I've had rope horses turn a corner, hit a slick spot and fall like a bomb. There's no time to get clear. These are unavoidable risks a trainer must take, but many people run their horses on wet ground, on pavement, on ice and snow. These are avoidable risks and foolish chances to take. Play it safe when footing is bad.

Getting kicked by a horse is almost always avoidable. Don't give that horse a chance to kick you. Even your gentle old pet will kick you if you startle him. Make a habit of talking, singing or whistling when you're around horses. At least they'll know you're there. Give those horses at sales and shows plenty of room and you'll stay healthier longer. If your horse develops the kicking habit, whip him hard when he does it. This is a dangerous habit.

Zorro's rearing horse looks pretty. So does Lone Ranger's and other movie and television horses. However, rearing is a very dangerous habit. If you have a rearing horse, get rid of him or take it out of him. He's a menace! One slip and he's over on you.

The bucking horse is dangerous. However, getting bucked down by your personal horse just shouldn't happen. The horses of "weekend" riders are apt to buck because they feel so good they just have to buck to get it out of their systems. A little exercise on a longe line or just turning the horse out in a pen for some play before a ride will save you some lumps.

Some people seem to use no judgment when riding horses. One fault I often see, in and out of the show ring, is riding too close behind another horse. I ride alongside or keep at least a horse's length between my horse and another horse. One horse length is the *minimum* distance. A novice should widen this gap. This is the distance for walking horses. It should increase with speed (as with autos). The distance it takes you to stop should be a good rule of thumb. A good cowboy friend, a regular he-wolf of a bronc rider, fractured his kneecap in seven places because the bronc he was riding was not well controlled. He ran up onto a gentle old horse, which kicked back hard. The bronc didn't do it; the old gentle horse did.

I often wonder why half the people and horses at shows and sales are not killed. Little children run under horses, people slap strange horses on the rump and riders act in the most reckless manner imaginable. Studs are tied up with light show halters and bridles. The result is always loose studs and injuries to horses and people. Stay with those horses when you are showing. I remember one time I didn't.

We were at a big show with a couple of halter horses. I had them in stalls but left them to grab a bite to eat. When I came back, I found part of a poison fly-bait in my filly's feed box. Probably some child thought it was candy and wanted to feed the "pretty horsie." The result was a scramble for a vet and then the antidote. We saved the filly, but it was close.

Did you ever have a mare chase you (when you were on horse-back) in a pasture? It goes like this—you take a short-cut through the horse pasture and an old cranky mare charges up to you, wheels and kicks you right off your horse.

I try never to go through a horse pasture unless I am riding a well-trained horse I can rope off. I carry my rope in a ready position so I can whop a mare if she decides to take my horse. A few sessions will generally break most mares of wanting to charge your saddle horse, but you never know. A horse is a big powerful animal, and a person is foolish to put himself, powerless to act, at a horse's mercy.

I always have a lot of studs in my training barn. I know for a fact that most small children that come into the barn will try to reach through the boards to pat a stud on the nose. I have the barn arranged so that this is impossible. Most horses are gentle, but there is always a risk.

With all these studs to train, I sometimes get too busy to take all the precautions I should. Remember, though, that these horses see me all the time and know I'm afraid of them. I know when a stud is feeling mischievous by his actions. You get a sixth sense after a lifetime of handling horses, and I am very cautious with a new stud until I know him. Remember that when you see a professional horseman handle a horse with recklessness and abandon, he knows the horse. Don't try it yourself. And one pro won't or shouldn't get fresh with another pro's horses.

Many people get hurt by riding too close to the arena gate. When the horse comes to the gate, instead of passing it he may pull in to get out of the arena. The result is a broken knee for the rider and a good chance of a broken leg for the horse. Don't lope by close to that gate.

The same thing goes for riding close to barbwire. A horse will sometimes almost go to sleep and hang the rider right in the wire. It cuts like a meat saw if you are traveling too fast. Another spooky thing is to have a horse switch his tail and catch it solidly on a barb. You're really "balling the jack" for a while. Stay away from barbwire, gates with bolts sticking out, vines you may tangle the horse in, holes he may fall into, roads he may slip on, studs, mares in a pasture, etc. Boil it all down and come up with one word—THINK.

13.

Preparing and Showing
Halter Horses

It's a credit to many judges that they'll place a poor showman once in a while. I can't understand why a person will haul
a horse to a show, pay an entry fee and then present the horse in
the poorest possible manner. It's as if the person wanted to lose.

You'll see horses in a halter class that haven't been cleaned up,
that are allowed to wander around and that are undisciplined.
When one of these horses gets a ribbon, you know that the judge
really liked that horse. I've seen judges jump around here and
there, making a supreme effort to look at a horse that won't stand
still.

But the horseman who cleans his horse, teaches him to stand
and teaches him some discipline will get far more ribbons and
trophies with the same kind of animals than the haphazard
showman.

Naturally, the horse must stand for the judge's inspection. The
horse must be alert, not asleep. When Mr. Judge moves to your
horse, have that horse ready, legs properly positioned and
alerted. Don't jump, crouch or wave your arms. Train the horse
so that when you slightly raise that lead shank and *look at him*,
he'll be alert. Teach the horse to watch you. If the man at the
lead shank must perform all sorts of antics to alert the horse, that
horse isn't ready to show.

I once had a colt that stood with his hind legs too close together. This was a natural stance for him, but he couldn't show
standing like that. We practiced at home until he knew that when
he was held and moved, he should stand with his legs square

under him. I didn't whip him, but I did jerk him a bit (lightly) with the lead chain over his nose. When he got sleepy with me, I'd jerk him awake. This shouldn't be overdone. Don't injure the nose. A light snap of the chain will wake up the horse. Jerk him back and he'll jump around, afraid and sore.

It's quicker to wash the colt and put some coat preparation on him than it is to brush him all the time. It'll get him cleaner, too. I like to wash the horse and blanket him the day before I haul him to a show. I keep with me a soft towel with some hair conditioner on it to polish him right before his class. I take the towel to the gate and work on him right up to show time. Many times a little cloud of dust will dirty him. You need that towel with you. Drop it at the gate when entering the ring and pick it up when retiring. The clean horse will impress the judge. He generally gives A for effort.

The hooves should be trimmed or shod. Oil or polish the hooves before showing.

Use a light, neat halter to show off a good head. Keep it simple. A stallion halter should be neat, but strong enough to cover any emergencies. A stallion should always be shown with the chain snapped on the right cheek ring of the halter, run across the nose, and out the left cheek ring. The chain over the nose will keep the horse down if he wants to rear up. You'll gain no points by not using the nose chain, for it's a matter of safety in a stallion class.

Many people use a tranquilizer on halter horses, especially young stallions. I have never done this but would certainly use the mild oral type if this were necessary for a particular horse. However, such use of tranquilizer on all one's horses only proves that one's horses aren't handled enough.

I make a practice of leading my halter horses from the right side. This serves a twofold purpose. First, since halter horses are paraded counter-clockwise, the judge sees all of my horse. I'm blocking no portion of my horse's anatomy. Second, I'm generally the only one doing this in a class. Since it's unusual, I have a better chance of getting the judge's attention.

I like to get my horse into the ring first. "The first look is the best look." The judge, in all probability, sees the first horse entering the ring the longest. I won't fight or endanger my horse by crowding into the ring first, but if I can get in without too much trouble, I'll always be in there first.

Nothing detracts more from a horse than a sloppy handler. Dress to fit the occasion. A new hat of popular style, good shined boots, correct attire plus a flawlessly groomed, well-mannered horse make for a winning combination. An unshaven, sloppily dressed person detracts from the horse and puts the whole show in a bad light.

I once was showing a nice colt by Poco Tivio. We had done fairly well all season and had hauled to the biggest show in the state, a Class A. There were about thirty-five horses in the two-year-old stallion class. I knew something about the judge but had never met him. He was an old cowboy, one of the Quarter Horse Association founders. I knew he liked Poco Tivio and also knew what an old cowboy like him liked to see in the show ring.

Most Quarter Horse men who have been around quite a while dislike gaudy western wear. Their idea of correct attire is a white arrow shirt, a plain necktie, clean Levi's of correct length, good polished boots and a good hat with a common sense crease. I so prepared myself.

My horse was cleaned and ready. I got through the gate first and led my horse from the right. I was pleased to note that the judge was looking at my horse.

When we lined up, I let the colt sleep until the judge neared me. I tapped the colt lightly on the nose to alert him and square him off. The judge looked him over. I moved quietly away so I never interfered with his line of vision, keeping the colt between me and the judge. He pulled the colt's tail and swung on it while looking at his hindquarters. Then I pulled a "sneaky." The judge backed away to look at the all-over picture of the colt. When he did this, I moved the colt a little, then said, "Whoa, Tivio!"

The judge perked up, looked at me and asked, "How's this ol' colt bred?"

Says I, "He's by Poco Tivio an' out of a Jimmy Reed mare."

"Sure, sure, he yipps, "he looks jus' like ol' Tivio."

With that I had the class won. We made Reserve Champion at that show, winning over some very tough horses.

Sneaky? Maybe. Crooked? No. I ended that season with a two-year-old colt that was Grand Champion Stallion for the state.

I didn't win them all that year, or any year. I never asked a judge *why* he placed me where he placed me. Some poor horses beat me. But I never fought with a judge. If I happened to be near a judge, I'd tell him that I thought he was doing a fine job and inquire about his health and his horses. Heck, he might be judging me again sometime.

I once hauled a filly five hundred miles to a show. She was good enough to be Reserve Champion mare for the state the year my two-year-old colt was Grand Champion Stallion. At this particular show I had her in a class of eight fillies and she never got a ribbon. Her next show saw her the class winner and Grand Champion Mare. I didn't discuss placings with either of the two judges.

I made a little show that a friend of mine was judging. He put my colt down to fourth and my filly down to third with some dogs beating me. That noon I saw him at the concession stand.

"Hey, ol' boy," says he, with enthusiasm, "them two horses you're hauling are about as good as any I ever seen."

Says I, less warmly, "Thanks, ol' buddy. How about a hot dog an' a Coke?"

Now any fool could have said, "Well, heck, if you like them so durn much, why'd you put them down?"

Yes, I thought of it and it was hard not to make some such retort. But if you want to win a ribbon once in a while, control your tongue and your temper. He may judge you again sometime, and he will certainly think of you in a more favorable light if you've been pleasant to him in the past. He'll not make you a winner if you've gone up to him, all foamy-mouthed, ranting at him about what a lousy judge he is.

Show these good horses right—in a professional manner—and you'll have some winners.

14.

Photographing the Western Horse

Maybe this subject doesn't really belong in a book on horse training, but for many years photography has played a large part in my training business. The trainer should produce some pictures of a horse working as a present for his client. This added service pleases customers, for I have never yet met a person who didn't like a nice picture of his horse.

It takes many years to learn enough about photography to make professional-looking pictures, especially of the working horse. Anyone can take a nice posed picture if a few simple rules are observed. More about this later.

There are many professional horse photographers who can make fine shots of your horses. They will do a superior job when compared to the professional photographer who takes *few* horse pictures—"there are tricks to all trades."

However, a professional horse photographer might not always be at your beck and call. An alternative suggestion is to locate a semi-professional. Many high schools and colleges teach photography. A technically proficient cameraman is available most anywhere. He should be easy to locate. Your camera store or photographic material supplier should be able to tell you about this. I would suggest lending the photographer this book so that he can read this section on some little tricks of the trade.

First, the single-lens reflex is the most practical camera to use. Such a camera allows the photographer to see the actual picture he's going to get. Interchangeable lenses are important, for the telephoto lens makes an undistorted picture possible.

We've all seen pictures of horses taken from the front that

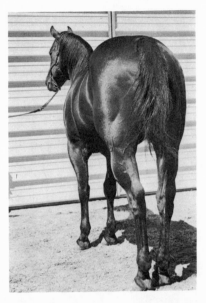 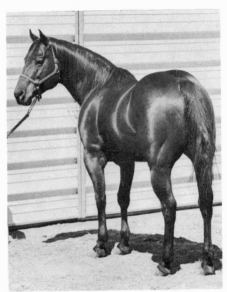

(Left): *The distorted picture we see so often in advertising pictures of Quarter Horses. A normal focal-length lens, used up close, will produce this abnormality. Many breeders think that this is the way to advertise a horse, but in reality, nothing can be learned from such a photograph. To correct this condition the photographer should either stand farther back and use his enlarger to get size in the picture or (preferably) use a telephoto lens.*

(Right): *King of Clubs (by King, out of Betty H by King). Though it's a fairly good picture, King could be standing a bit better—he's posed too wide behind, and stands too narrow in front. A 135mm lens (almost 3X) was used to eliminate distortion, and a polarizing filter was used to eliminate reflected glare from the barn doors.*

show a huge head and forequarters, with the rear end tapering off to nothing. This fault is due to the photographer's use of a normal-length lens and being too near the horse when taking pictures. He should have stayed back from the horse and had the picture cropped and enlarged in the darkroom, or he could have used a telephoto lens which would have kept the horse in correct proportion.

The correct focal length for horse photography is important. I believe that ½ to 3-power is about right. The normal focal length lens for the 35mm camera is generally about 50mm. The telephoto length I like best is 135mm when using the 35mm camera. Anything shorter produces distortion. A longer telephoto lens produces a shortening effect, making the horse look, from the front, as though his head is too small and his back too short. And the longer the focal length, the less depth of field—meaning the photographer using a 300mm lens might get the head in sharp focus while the rear of the horse would be out of focus. Depth of field is very important in action photography, for the rapidly moving horse can easily work out of focus.

A shutter speed of at least 1/500th second should be used to take action pictures unless some intentional blurring (to show movement) is desired. The horse, moving directly across the field of view, will get a little blur in the legs at 1/1000th second. Action is more easily stopped with the horse coming in the direction of the camera.

Background is very important. The posed horse should have a contrasting background. The dark horse requires a light background; a light horse, a dark background. The light background is suitable for the majority of horse pictures. A white barn (no distracting windows or doors, please), a picture against the sky or a prepared background such as painted plywood are all very good.

Posing the horse requires practice by the horse-owner. It's difficult to get a good picture when the horse fidgets and moves around. A good way to practice is to use a stallion show halter with the chain of the lead shank running over the horse. If the horse moves forward, a sharp, easy jerk on the chain should make him stand. Pet him as a reward for being still. Make him stand for a few minutes at a time.

The extremely nervous horse that just can't stand still can be tranquilized with such a medication as oral Sparine. The photographer should shoot many pictures (at least twenty exposures) of such a horse. The least expected exposure will often show off such a horse to good advantage even though he isn't posed exactly right.

The horse pictures from the side (a preferred view) must show

Here is King as seen from the side view. His legs are all right, his head is up and angled slightly toward the camera so that both ears show. He's holding his tail well, too. All in all, an alert expression.

all four legs. The legs toward the camera should be in their natural position, while the legs away from the camera should show *between* the near legs. Just a small separation of near and off leg is all that's necessary. A large separation looks awkward. This might sound difficult but a horse moves in this manner. To get correct leg position, just move the horse forward or back a step or two.

Pictures from the front or rear should show all legs straight down from the body. The legs should appear *firmly* planted. This is generally a bit more difficult than the side view.

The horse should look alert, ears forward and tail held out from the body. Alerting the horse without frightening him out of position is trying on the horse, owner and photographer. A third person, the horse "alerter," is almost always needed.

Waving a handkerchief or sack might work for a picture or two. Opening and closing an umbrella often gets results when all else fails. When nothing seems to work, another horse can be led around or held just where the photographer wants the subject to look. Think about it and you can come up with many different things to alert the horse.

The horse should be neat and clean—really shined up for his photograph. Keeping a light sheet on him really improves his coat. Trim out the ears and trim the fetlocks and the backs of the legs. Comb and brush the mane and tail. There are prepared shampoose and coat conditioners available. A fly repellent is a must, for the horse can't stand still if he's crawling with flies.

Many of you would like to take a good picture of your horse and have no expensive camera with an assortment of lenses. You can do a good job if you realize your limitations and the limitations of your camera.

First, clean that horse as though a top photographer with his $1,000 camera was coming to make the picture. Second, make the photo by sunlight, a bright sun, and in the early morning or late afternoon when the sun furnishes you with a strong sidelight. The noon sun overhead presents shadows that give an untrue representation of the horse.

Third, study the direct side view and take only that pose. Even the head should point directly forward, or only *slightly* inclined toward the camera; just enough to show both ears and a slight bulge to indicate the off eye. This side view will be a correct, undistorted picture and the only one you should attempt without a telephoto lens.

Now, some technical stuff for the semi-pro.

You should process your own film if you use a 35mm camera. Commercial processing is too poor to produce good results unless you send the film to a custom lab. At the present time (film developers and papers are constantly being improved upon) I use Tri-X film, rate it at ASA 1200 and develop in Acufine. My favorite enlarging paper in Luminos and I use the F-3 grade, which gives the prints a lot more snap and helps fade out distracting background.

High-speed Ektachrome does a nice job of rendering correct horse color and works fine for color action. Grass and trees look natural. However, the sky comes out blank unless a polarizing filter is used. Kodachrome II is tops. Kodacolor is a good film to use for horse color. It's very versatile. It's a negative color film made primarily for color prints but beautiful slides are another result. Top quality black and white prints can be made from Kodacolor negatives by using Kodak's Panalure paper. *Caution:* Watch your darkroom safelight. Best results are accomplished by enlarging without a safelight and developing in darkness. A safelight can be used for the stop and fixing baths. There is a special safelight for Panalure, but it's so dim I'd as soon work in total darkness.

Dust is a problem in horse action photography. I suggest not using too long a telephoto. Get closer to the action or you'll get hazy pictures. Cuting horses really stir up a fog unless the arena is dampened. You have to stay back some distance to insure getting both horse and cow in the picture. Study cutting pictures to know what you're trying to take. You must know enough about the sport to be able to anticipate the blocks. The correct time to take the picture is when the horse turns the cow. The more violent the action, the better the shot. Shoot a lot of pictures. If you get one great picture out of thirty-six exposures, you're a real pro.

Getting a good roping picture is an art. Side views are pretty well out after the roper has stepped down because the length of rope between horse and calf is too great. Shoot with the action coming toward you with a slight angle to picture the whole horse and calf. The calf shouldn't block out any part of the horse. Make sure the rope is light-colored so it will show up clearly in the finished print.

There are different phases of action to capture when taking roping pictures. The rope about to settle around the calf's neck is good. Jerking the slack and pitching it away is always a favorite of ropers. The quick dismount with the horse sliding is tops. The moment the calf is jerked backward with the horse sliding and the roper getting down can't be beat. Pictures of the roper throwing the calf and tying it down are all right in a series but are nothing you'd make a special effort to take. And the rope horse breaking from the box makes an interesting picture.

There are only a few pictures that show off a reining horse. The slide and the spin predominate. The spin is *very* difficult to cap-

One of the best moments to stop rope-horse action—the rope has just looped over the calf, and the slack is about to be jerked up.

ture. I'd shoot a full roll and pick the best shot. Shoot from the side or slightly to the front of the background you want. Shoot the slide from the side or slightly to the front. A low camera angle will accentuate the action from the front view. Sliding pictures are tough only because there are so few horses that do a good slide. If the arena is dusty, wait until the dust settles between each shot. A little dust will accentuate the action.

A general rule is that all horse pictures should be taken from eye level. Never get down low when taking a *posed* picture. The horse will look unnatural. It lengthens the legs, gives the horse a big-bellied appearance and makes all horses look like they're too shallow through the flank. Shooting down makes a horse look too short.

I make contact sheets, study the shots with a magnifying glass and print only the best ones. This saves time and money. Why print bad pictures? There are too many bad horse pictures floating around now. I hope that this advice helps people make better ones!

Questions and Answers

*My horse takes the left lead readily, but not the right.
What can I do?*

Start your horse in a lope in a small circle to the right.
You can force the lead by scaring the horse into the right lead.
Hold the reins in your right hand and use a bat forcefully on the
left shoulder. Practice small circles at a lope every day. The
first day, ride about five to eight small circles, then increase the
number daily. Use leg pressure when you do this. Left leg for
right lead. Circle about three times as many circles on the bad
lead as on the good lead.

If you cannot get the horse to take the lead at all, start by
longeing the horse to the right. Forget the circles to the left until
the right lead comes easily and naturally.

*My horse holds his head away from the direction he is
going when I neck-rein him. He gets worse the faster
he works. It there any way to correct this?*

This is a common fault with horses that have been carelessly
neck-reined. To get him over this, he must have his head pulled
into correct position with a direct rein. A colt bit or double bridle
should be used for this. A hackamore can be used if the horse will
work all right in one. Never pull directly on the curb bit rein.
Leg pressure should be used to help correct the horse.

The horse carrying his head away from his turns cannot watch
the ground and so may fall. He certainly isn't supple. He's the
opposite of supple, whatever that is. This is a fairly hard condition to correct. Training bridles must be used even though you
cannot use this type of gear at a show.

*All my horse wants to do is run. He pulls on the bit so
hard that my arms ache from holding him in. His head
is so high he cannot watch the ground. He was not like
this when I got him. What can I do with him? Should I
buy a more severe bit?*

No, a severe bit isn't the answer. Circling in an arena will often
slow down such a horse. Something such as a running martingale,
draw reins or a corrective tie-down should be used to lower his
head. Let him run in small circles in the pen until he slows down.
If he never slows down, you have been made a fool of and the
best thing would be to forget this horse and try another.

You have made this horse foolish by running him to the barn.
Perhaps you have raced to the barn with another horse. Speed
has come down on him. You held him in by brute force instead
of correcting the condition. This has made him more silly as he
has learned that it's all right to go back to his stall as fast as he
can get there. You have confused him by holding him in. Correction is a long, slow, often unrewarding proposition. When you
get your next horse, remember always to walk back to the barn.

*Some people claim that you can't ride properly in any-
thing but a "balanced ride" saddle, and others say that
this is just a lot of nonsense, and that a saddle is a
matter of personal choice. Who is right?*

Through the years I've sat in just about every kind of saddle you can think of. I've had some long rides in those little
English postage stamps, some mighty short ones in Association rigs
and I've tried most everything in between. In the end (if you'll excuse the expression) I've got to agree that the choice of a saddle
depends partly on what you're going to use it for, partly on how
it fits you and your pony and mostly on what you have learned to
like.

The balanced ride was partially invented by Monte Foreman.
I say "partially invented" because there's nothing new about his
saddle. He has reworked and combined old proven appointments
into a new concept in saddlery. I would condense the explanation
by describing the "balanced ride" as a "dressage saddle with a
horn."

This saddle is gaining wide popularity. It allows the rider to maintain a natural position, almost identical to the balanced seat one must assume when riding bareback. Almost everyone rides better when using this saddle.

The two most important features of the saddle are:

(1) The seat is level. The rider can assume a natural seat without being *forced* back on the cantle.

(2) The stirrups are hung about four inches farther forward than on a conventional stock saddle. Without this, feature number one would be nullified.

I've heard this saddle described as a "forward seat." It is not a forward seat. It is truly a balanced ride. A conventional saddle could easily and accurately be described as a "backward ride."

If a rider has ridden the regular stock saddle all of his life, the balanced ride takes a little getting used to. Many people ride a fairly short stirrup, and this doesn't work with the Foreman saddle. I like to be able to just move a little to stand up. I'm almost standing when I'm normally working a horse.

The extremely long stirrup keeps you in a balanced position all the time. If a colt shies or bucks, the rider is already positioned to "go with him." This is a very *secure* seat. It takes only a little effort to "lock on." If there were no other advantages to this saddle, this alone would make it worth using. The rider can always ride better if he has confidence in being able to stay on the horse. Falls are unpleasant and dangerous.

When working the colt, the balanced seat, weight in the stirrups, puts the weight of the rider about six inches in back of the withers. This is where the horse can best carry weight. He can't do his best with weight over his kidneys. Forward weight allows him to get the necessary arch in his back and to get those hind legs up under him as, in a natural fashion, he is able to.

The saddle has the rigging built into the skirts. This eliminates unnecessary bulk and allows the rider to get closer to the horse. Rigging in the skirts also has the advantage of "wrapping the skirts around the horse," which holds the saddle more firmly to the horse.

Are there disadvantages to this saddle?

The only one that I can see is that the rider who's used to sitting down and relaxing, as if in an easy chair, won't like this saddle. You ride "straight up," weight in the stirrups, ready for anything. Is such riding tiring?

No, I don't think so. The conventional saddle forces a horse to carry weight over a spot that's tiring for him. He's a fresher horse when he carries weight where it's easiest for him. Nothing wearies a rider more than legging a tired horse along. The fresh horse always relaxes the rider.

Most people resist change. They go along with "fads" but seldom agree with new concepts. I don't think that the western riding world will *universally* accept the Foreman saddle. I can work a horse better and am safer when riding this saddle. I'd use no other. After using Monte's saddle for many years, the conventional saddle feels like a "freak."

How can I teach my horse to ground-tie?

Ground-tying is, I believe, a bad practice. At best, the horse may step on a rein, jerk back and injure his mouth. At it's worst, the horse may "untrain" himself and leave you afoot in a bad spot.

If you're training for a trail horse class, however, there are several ways to go about this. Wrap some rubber around the bit to pad it. Tie it in place. A piece of inner tube is all right.

Take some sticks and baling wire. Form a loop about a foot or so above the stick with the wire wrapped around the middle of the stick. Bury these sticks all over your place with the wire loop (small) exposed. Ride to them and tie up. Stay close and have a sharp knife handy in case of a storm. Or carry a weight tied to a rein. Ride along, step off and drop the weighted rein. Or tie the rein to the horse's pastern. I've used this method in an emergency. If I have to get off with no hobbles and no place to tie to, I will tie the rein to the pastern, long enough not to cause discomfort but short enough that the horse will pull and stop himself if he tries to get away. (This is illustrated in a painting by Charlie Russell, entitled, if I recall correctly, "Innocent Allies." A horse is so secured while his owner robs a stagecoach.)

My colt hates to lead and will travel sideways and toss his head continually. Then he will keep biting at the shank and eventually my hand to get his own way. He is very headstrong and will balk a great deal when leading. He has improved somewhat as I work with him every day and try to get his confidence. He used to rear up and fight me. He got over that but still pulls and bites the shank.

Also, he charges when we are at liberty in a ring. I can lead him on a long line in a field and he behaves fairly, but will run up close to me. He is not mean but wants to play; I have slapped him and used a switch to stop the charging, but it only makes him mad and hard to handle. Now I just push him away, and he just goes by me not trying to hurt me. Is there some way to stop this? I sent him to a professional trainer who did help somewhat, but all these habits are still with him. He is sixteen months old and will be gelded in about two months, which I am told will help settle him down, but perhaps there is some training I can give him to improve his manners.

I think your decision to geld your colt is very wise. However, I see no reason to wait two months. Certainly, two months' more development will be insignificant when compared to the chance you are now taking of being badly injured by this colt. If it is a question of castration during the summer because of fly infestation, there are certainly enough good fly repellents on the market to keep him fly-free. My best advice to you is to geld him immediately. I never like to see a girl handle a gentle stud, to say nothing of a firecracker such as you have.

This is an interesting problem. Let's forget that you plan to geld this colt and treat it as if you plan on keeping him unaltered. First, what is wrong? (1) Overfeeding? (2) Breeding? (3) Methods of correction?

(1) I suspect, though I certainly don't know, that you are taking *too* good care of your horse. The saying "feeling his oats" applies here, I believe. Today, the saying might be "feeling his sweet feed mix, vitamin, mineral and protein supplements." My

opinion is that most horses do not need much of this stuff. I think a supplement may be in order for brood stock and for the stallion during periods of heavy service. Also, an area may be deficient in certain minerals. Check with your county agent and your vet about this.

People always comment about how good the horses look in my barn. Horses come in for me to train that have been fed everything the owner could buy. I feed crimped oats and wheat bran, two parts oats to one part bran. I hay my horses a half-hour or so before I grain. Fresh water and salt are available at all times. The horses here start to pick up and look in condition soon. I'll tell you my secret ingredient—it's those damp saddle blankets.

(2) There are many horses that act like your colt and aren't overfed. I have trained many of them. These colts generally give a lot of trouble until they are old enough for a stiff ride. They have excess energy, are very mischievous and need to work this off. Certain bloodlines often produce these traits. I think your colt is this type of horse.

(3) You are certainly not punishing your colt when you hit him with your hand or a switch—but a real whipping would only make this colt worse. He'll fight you if you whip him.

The colt obviously needs restraint—so restrain him. Tie him up for a couple hours every day. When you do this, don't hover over him and untie him at the least little disturbance. Tie him in a safe place and let him have it out. Keep a sharp knife handy in case he gets in a serious jam. Stay someplace where you can keep an eye on him but where he can't see you.

Opinions vary on the correct methods to tie up horses. I like to tie at least five feet high. I personally prefer a strong soft rope. tied around the neck with a bowline (knot that won't slip) and run through the halter. The place you tie should have nothing that the colt can get his legs through and get caught.

It would be a good idea to break this colt to hobbles. Use a soft, strong hobble like the "Utah." A man should help you with this.

Tie a soft rope to the hobbles and spill the colt if he tries to fight or run on the hobbles. This is best done in a breaking pen with soft ground, where injury to the colt is less likely. (The run-

Questions and Answers   173

ning-W could also be used, but hobbles are simpler.) He should give up to this treatment very shortly, for it isn't intelligence he lacks.

I would suggest handling this colt with a snug hackamore, a California hackamore of braised rawhide, at least a half-inch in diameter. He can't bite much if the hackamore is snug enough. This makes a fine outfit to longe a colt with if you add a fiador (throatlatch). If you have to use a whip to longe the colt, however, I would use some other form of exercise such as ponying or exercise in a large pen. I hope the colt has a place to take his own exercise.

When visitors call, don't take them in the stallion's stall or pen, for he will soon be all over you wanting to bite. It's best not to fool around with a stallion (any stallion) very long.

You should get the stallion out, clean him quickly and start his work. You can pet and fool around with a mare or gelding. Not so the stallion. Give him no opportunity to bite. If you have to punish him, let him know it. Don't just peck at him.

I recall the first horse of this sort that was brought to me to train. Telling you about him may help you with your horse.

He was a line-bred, two-year-old stallion. He was broke to lead and that was all. He was always hungry for a meat diet—fingers, arms, etc. If you hit him for biting, he would rear up striking and come at you. He knew he'd be punished so he'd snap and fly back. Putting a halter on him was like hitting the beach on D-day.

I don't think any horse ever scared me more than he did. You'd have to be there to believe how rank this colt was. But I was being paid to ride him, so I hobbled him, first tying up a back foot, got the saddle and hackamore on him. I had no help so I couldn't drive him first. I was afraid he'd get all tangled up and rope-burned.

I got a short hold on the left rein, found the stirrup and started up. He reared up, struck but missed and went to spinning and snapping. He tore the shirt right off my back. If I had had a bad heart, I would have died right then.

But when I got on him and set, he walked off as if he had been ridden for a year. I never taught a colt, before or after, as much in one ride as I then taught that colt. I broke him to death. He liked to learn, for one thing, and I was scared to get off, for the other. He would roll-back, back fast and straight, lope in small circles and even figure-eight. When I did get off, he was gentle.

I tried to train him to stand still for me to get on. I put him in his stall, which was very large, and tried to get on and off him. He got worse. He'd try to slam himself against the wall to pin my leg. I decided that the best thing I could do was to ride him a lot and not try to train him except when riding him. He got over being bad to get on as soon as I stopped trying to train him. His formula was: saddle up, work, get off and leave him alone. With enough work he developed into a fairly gentle horse, and a regular Einstein of a horse when working.

I bought a nice reining horse that worked so well that I managed to win a few shows right after I bought him. Now he won't stop right, won't roll-back and never changes leads behind in a figure eight. He seems to get worse all the time, even though I practice the reining pattern over and over every day. What can I do to get this horse winning again?

The key to the answer lies in the part of the question that states that you "practice the reining pattern over and over every day." Any horse will go sour with such fare. This horse is sour from getting that pattern drilled into him daily.

The horse must have a variety of work to do anything well. This horse should have some pasture riding. You must give him something to look forward to. Once in awhile you can slide and roll-back around a tree, then figure-eight around an old log.

Working cattle would give this horse a reason for quick stops and turns. I'd suggest that you do some of this. Work a cow in the pen head to head, picking her off the fence each way. Hold her in a corner. Your horse will surprise you with his perfect changes of leads, his quick starts and fast getaways. Horses like playing with a cow. Dry reining practice is a bore for them.

No matter what I try, I can't catch my mare in the pasture. She runs around me and stops, leting me get close to her, then runs away. It generally takes me all afternoon to catch her. I'm then too tired and disgusted to ride. Is there any way to catch this mare and retain my sanity?

Many pros say never to feed a horse from your hand. I do feed horses from my hand as a reward. When I go into the pasture after a horse, I stand a lot better chance of catching that horse if he knows he'll get a bite of something he likes when I catch him. He'll never let me catch him if I chase him all over the place, getting angrier all the time.

It's true that some horses will just never let you catch them in the pasture. But you can build a trap in the time it takes to finally wear a horse down by running him.

The trap should be built on a fence line and have both entrance and exit. The gates should be left open except when actually trapping the horse. The trap funnels down at the exit so one person can crowd and catch a horse. The trap should be stout enough so that the horse can't injure himself or break out.

Salt should always be kept in the trap, and it's a good thing if the horse must enter the trap to drink. He gets so used to the trap that it's no great thing to trap him. After he's caught, he should be rewarded with a little food. He'll catch easier next time.

I recently bought a horse who cribs and sucks wind. How can I cure him of this vice?

I don't believe cribbing is really that much of a vice, but it's sure a provoking habit; there is nothing like a big windsucking gasp to frazzle and fray nerves to the breaking point.

I've heard all the old cures such as filing between the teeth and pulling a tooth. I've painted stalls with creosote, oil and grease. I've used neck straps, and they've helped on some. But when you get a real old-fashioned cribber, there's only one thing that will work. I've tried it and found it one hundred per cent effective. Just take everything out of the stall that a horse can crib on.

This is not quite as tough as it seems. The stall must be a box stall with no surface for the teeth to grip. Mangers and feed boxes come out. We can nail tin over wooden edges, letting it slope steeply to offer no grip for the teeth. We feed the horse in a nose-bag or a bucket, and we'll remove them after the horse has finished his meal. Salt and minerals that the horse would get from what we would place in his feed box are fed in the removable object we use, or given loose in a removable box. A bad cribber will even crib on a salt block.

We've effected no cure, but by golly the horse isn't cribbing, so it's the next best thing.

Perhaps we're too busy to take time to remove the feedbox or nosebag and must feed the horse in a permanent feed box. We can affix rollers over the exposed edges of the box that will turn and afford no grip for the teeth. Metal rollers are best, such as are used in grain crushing machinery.

If it's necessary to leave a feed box and manger in the stall, there's no way to do this. Hardly any cribber can crib on anything *below his knee*. Keep the feed box and manger right on the ground and he can't crib. He can, however, chew wood, so metal boxes seem to be the best in the long run.

Most horses that crib, chew wood and stall-weave are all nervous horses. They never seem to be good in a stall. They need something to keep them interested. I've seen an old basketball hung with a rope run through it help such a horse. However, it's hard on a person's nerves to listen to a horse continually bumping that ball. A goat as a companion is often a fine remedy. A pony is a companion to many a thoroughbred. If a horse is interested in anything but his bad habit, he may quit it.